AMERICAN HISTORY MYSTERIES

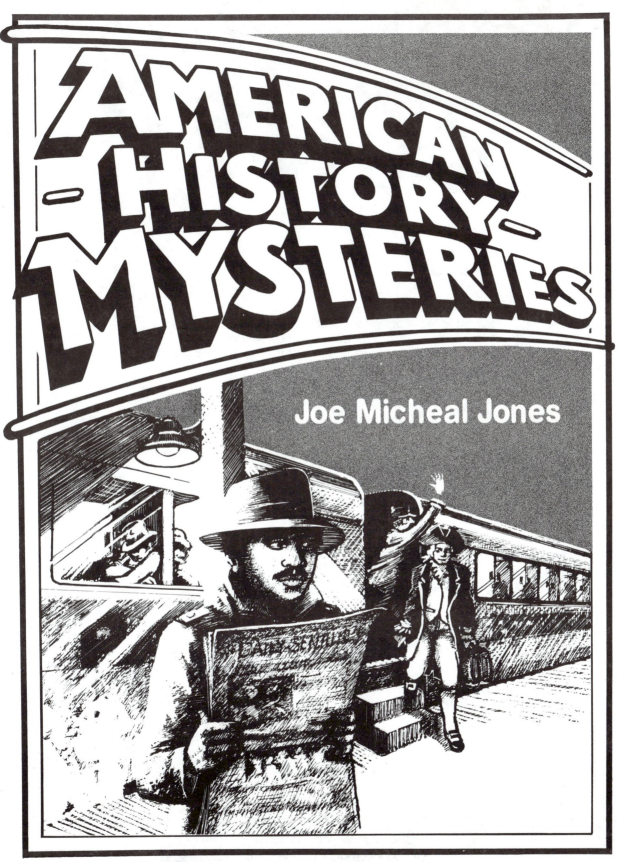

Joe Micheal Jones

 J. Weston Walch, Publisher

Portland, Maine

1   2   3   4   5   6   7   8   9   10

01-7100

ISBN 0-8251-1567-1

Copyright © 1989
J. Weston Walch, Publisher
P.O. Box 658 • Portland, Maine 04104-0658

Printed in the United States of America

Contents

Mystery Story Numbers	I. Colonial Period	Page Numbers

II. Revolution

III. Constitution

Teacher Introduction

American History Mysteries are a proven classroom aid for American history. They have almost unlimited potential due to their flexibility. They can be used to introduce a unit of study or to check understanding of a unit just completed. They are very useful in helping to stimulate research on the various people or periods covered by the story, and they can also get students interested in writing their own "mysteries." Mysteries spark discussion and sharpen logical and critical thinking skills. Best of all, students find them fun to solve. The stories are based on historical fact, so students learn history while having fun.

The stories in this book are arranged according to historical periods (see Table of Contents). Mysteries 1–50 usually require more historical knowledge than the average student would possess. An encyclopedia or other reference book, plus some careful thought on the student's part, will enable that student to successfully solve the mystery. Mysteries 51–100 are geared to the younger or less capable student. They use basically the same story, but the clues are easier and more obvious. Teachers are thus able to use these stories with various grades and achievement levels. The student introduction is the same for both levels.

Many stories have suggestions for further study. They go a little deeper into the topic of the story and are intended to help the teacher broaden the scope of the lesson. For the most part, though, students' questions that always arise after using these stories will be springboard enough to launch you into a more detailed study.

Each teacher has permission to photocopy these stories for use in his or her classroom. Because many teachers have limited resources, these stories are structured in such a way as to give each teacher maximum flexibility. Some teachers may want to give each student his or her own copy to keep and use. Other teachers may want to keep classroom copies for use by other classes too. With this in mind, you should give specific instructions to your students before they begin to use the stories. Students should understand the following before they begin:

1. The student introduction

2. Whether they may write on the stories

3. Whether they must include source information with the answer

4. Any other specific information you may require from them

The answers to the Mysteries follow this teacher introduction. Please see note at the beginning of the Table of Contents.

Answer Section

1. Hail Columbia

Columbus never actually landed at Washington, D.C. As a matter of fact, he never even laid eyes on any part of what is now the United States. He landed on San Salvador and most of the islands lying off the continent, including Cuba, the Bahamas, and Haiti.

Further Information:

After Columbus's first trip, Queen Isabella treated him as a hero, but when he failed to turn up the riches of the Orient after three more voyages, he was disgraced. After his fourth voyage he lived out his remaining life in poverty and obscurity.

For Further Study:

1. Why do we honor Columbus so if he never even saw the United States?

2. Why was he treated as a failure when he returned to Spain?

3. Where did the name America come from?

4. Have there been others whose contribution was not recognized in their own lifetime?

2. Live and Let Live

In our early Colonial days most religions were very intolerant of others. For example, the Massachusetts Puritans believed that religious toleration was a dangerous weakness inspired by the devil. They banished Roger Williams and Anne Hutchinson, but these two fared better than Quakers who settled in their colony—some of them were hanged on Boston Common. Virginia, on the other hand, expelled Massachusetts preachers who came there to preach. It should be noted, however, that Roger Williams went on to found Rhode Island—by far the most tolerant colony. In time, all the colonies developed religious toleration.

For Further Study:

1. Why did toleration develop here in a relatively short time?

2. Is it now developing or will it develop in the Middle East and elsewhere?

3. Where is there severe religious conflict in the world now?

3. Who's Number One?

The first permanent settlement in what is now the U.S. was at St. Augustine. The first permanent English settlement was at Jamestown, Virginia—not at Plymouth.

For Further Study:

1. The Roanoke colony will be brought up by the students. The fate of this colony is still a mystery and should lead to interesting conversation, speculation, and research.

2. The types of government that these settlements had would be a good research topic. Students could debate the weak and strong points of the different governments. It should be interesting to see if the students could determine why the settlers had the form of government they did. Would they be the same today?

3. What makes people want to leave their homes and venture into the unknown?

4. What were the priorities of the settlers in this new land? What would they be on the moon? What things would remain a concern of people settling the moon?

4. The Incident in Boston

Sally meant that many facts were left out of Jackson's explanation, just as they were left out of the reports of the incident when it occurred. The truth was that the crowd became quite large and had forced the small group of soldiers up against a wall. With nowhere to escape to, they felt their lives were endangered—and opened fire. It is unclear whether they were given the order to fire or whether they simply panicked. Nevertheless, Samuel Adams used the incident to create great excitement and much hostility against the British when he reported it in a pamphlet and distributed it all over the colonies. It was a powerful propaganda tool against England.

Semantics as used here refers to the use of the word "massacre" in an attempt to create the desired effect upon the reader. The Boston "Incident" would never have achieved the same degree of emotional involvement as the Boston "Massacre."

For Further Study:

1. Have students look into other uses of propaganda and semantics.

2. Is propaganda wrong?

3. How effective is it?

4. Look for examples of it in history and advertising.

5. Review the merits of substituting one word for another as to people's reactions to them. Examples: *quiz* for test, *loss* for death, *roared* for cheered, *wailing* for crying.

5. Ben and Bill

He meant that someone who knew as much about Franklin as the driver did must also know that his birthplace was in Boston, not Philadelphia. He must have been trying to run up the cab fare by suggesting a trip to Franklin's birthplace, therefore making him untrustworthy.

For Further Study:

Have the students prepare an even more detailed report on Franklin's many accomplishments. They were many and varied. Examples:

1. He had only two years of formal schooling, but did not let that stop him from becoming a lifelong learner.

2. He had a state names after him, but it was never admitted to the union. It consisted of part of Tennessee and North Carolina.

3. His funeral was attended by at least half of the entire city of Philadephia.

6. Bunker Hill

The Battle of Bunker Hill was fought on June 17, 1775, but the actual battle took place on Breed's Hill, adjacent to Bunker Hill. During the night of June 16, Colonel William Prescott sent his men to fortify Bunker Hill, but by mistake they fortified Breed's Hill.

The next day the British decided to drive the Americans away. The red-coats were twice repulsed with heavy losses, but a third attack forced the Americans back (they had exhausted their powder). Although it was a loss for the Americans militarily, it was a moral victory. It showed that Americans could and would stand up to British regulars.

British losses were about 1000 men—more than double the American losses. One eighth of all British officers that fell in the Revolutionary War fell at this battle.

For Further Study:

1. Find the names of the men prominent in this battle and follow them through the war.

2. Compile a list of battles won and lost for the Americans. It should be interesting, because we lost more than we won. Why then are we free?

7. The Wax Museum

Washington's biographer, James Thomas Flexner, holds that Washington's teeth were not wooden. They were hippopotamus ivory. He also had porcelain ones. Wooden teeth could possibly have been used for a very short period of time.

8. Georgia Peach

Georgia had no representative at the First Continental Congress.

9. A Rough Copy

No. Jefferson's original rough draft used the word "inalienable." When the document was copied in the official version, the word became "unalienable."

10. United We Stand

First of all, the states were anything but united. Most historians agree that slightly more than one third of the population supported independence, slightly less than one third supported England, and about one third were neutral. Without help from France, and England's involvement in wars in Europe, it might have been impossible for us to gain independence.

Secondly, important battles were fought all over the country, even in territories that were not states yet.

For Further Study:

1. How much help did we get from outside?

2. Why was there such division in the country?

3. In how many different states did battles take place?

4. Were attitudes different in the different sections of the country? Why?

11. A College Education

Up through the 1984 election we have had three presidents elected by the Electoral College with fewer popular votes than their closest opponent. They are John Q. Adams, 1824; Rutherford B. Hayes, 1876; and Benjamin Harrison, 1888.

For Further Study:

1. Debate the merits of an electoral college system versus direct election of our president.

2. Note how the system has been changed over the years by parties and amendments.

3. The elections of 1800, 1824, and 1876 are especially interesting. Look at them in particular.

4. Does your state require by law that electors vote as directed by the peoples' ballots? Should it?

12. Jefferson Papers

Thomas Jefferson was not at the Constitutional Covention. Jefferson served as Minister to France from May 1784 until November 1789. The Constitution went into effect after its adoption by New Hampshire (the ni state to do so) on June 21, 1788. Jefferson had been sent a Constitution by James Madison and he did approve it.

to the lack of a bill of rights and actively urged adoption of one. North Carolina and Rhode Island refused to approve the Constitution until Congress agreed to add a bill of rights.

13. Right Man for the Job

The Constitution gives *no* requirement at all for justices of the Supreme Court, so a person's judicial experience does not count.

14. A Judicial Review

The Constitution does not directly grant the power of judicial review. This is one of the things that has been established through time and is now accepted. Also, the Constitution gives several checks of Supreme Court power.

15. A Little Knowledge

The founding fathers felt that a bill of rights was not necessary. Americans had a long governmental tradition of personal liberties, and the founding fathers felt that they were well known. Furthermore, every state constitution had a bill of rights. The federal Constitution would not make these rights null and void. Most founding fathers simply felt that a bill of rights was not needed for the above reasons. Curry knew a bill of rights was not included but did not know why. That caused him to make wrong assumptions and false generalizations— dangerous for any teacher.

For Further Study:

1. Have students research the Constitutional Convention to find the behind-the-scenes activities that went on, such as the debate on a bill of rights. They will find it interesting.

2. Discuss reasons for the tough time the Constitution had being ratified. What were people's objections to it?

   ⸱⸱cisms of the Constitution concerning slavery and other topics.

   ⸱ ⸱⸱ history seen through today's eyes is often
   ⸱ther's eyes in a different time with

5. Research Charles Beard's *An Economic Interpretation of the Constitution*. It has been pretty much refuted by now, but it is still interesting.

16. English Ingenuity

Our earliest factories were textile related and did come from England, but their technology was hardly "freely shared" with us. England wanted to protect its own industries from competition. Therefore it was illegal for most textile workers to leave the country, for they would take knowledge of how the machinery worked with them. Industrial technology was closely guarded and none was to be exported to America or anywhere else. Samuel Slater, the father of the American factory system, was an Englishman attracted to America by the high bounties being offered here to anyone with industrial knowledge. He memorized the plans for an entire spinning factory and escaped to New York in disguise. Moses Brown, a Rhode Island Quaker and capitalist, backed Slater financially and they built the factory there.

For Further Study:

1. Others brought technology to America, too. Examples are the Scholfield brothers, Paul and Arthur, and Francis Cabot Lowell, an American who smuggled plans for a power loom out of England. See what information the class can find on these men and others.

2. We also had many great American inventors: Eli Whitney, Elias Howe, Isaac Singer, Oliver Evans, Benjamin Franklin—the list goes on and on. Have the class find information on American inventors and inventions.

3. Have students make a list of things they would like to see invented. See if anyone can come up with plans for his or her invention.

4. Find out why the North became so much more industrialized than the South.

5. What industries are in the local area? Who started them? When?

17. Old Hickory

Jackson's wife died before the inauguration so she could not have worn the brooch as First Lady in the White House.

For Further Study:

Have students do further research on Jackson. His storied military career was fascinating, as was most everything else about him. Explore his background, personality, and the election of 1824 "corrupt bargain," as well as his presidency and all the changes it brought to American politics.

18. New Orleans

The Battle of New Orleans took place on January 8, 1815. The Treaty of Ghent, the peace treaty ending the War of 1812, was signed on December 24, 1814. The war was over before the Battle of New Orleans was fought. Lack of effective communications resulted in America's greatest victory of the war and made Andrew Jackson a national hero and most probably president a few years later. Officially, though, the war was already over. Nevertheless, Americans took great pride in the victory.

19. *Old Ironsides*

Old Ironsides had wooden sides. Its name came when most of the *Guerriere's* shells bounced off her sides as if they were iron.

20. Captain Ghost

Robert E. Lee was not present at First Manassas. General Pierre G.T. Beauregard was in command there, and with help from General Joseph E. Johnston he defeated the Union forces under General Irvin McDowell in the first major battle of the war.

For Further Study:

Look at the personal side of the war. Lee was offered command of all the Union armies but could not bring himself to oppose his friends and family and his native state. He was serving as military advisor to President Jefferson Davis during this battle. He took command of the Army of Northern Virginia on June 1, 1862, after General Johnston was wounded.

Do a study on personal reasons for taking sides in the war. Lincoln's wife had several brothers fighting for the South. Senator Crittenden of Kentucky had two sons, one a general for the South, the other a general for the North. Have them find other examples.

21. Thanks But No Thanks

President Buchanan was our only bachelor President so he could not have given a doll to his daughter.

22. Mr. Lincoln

The Emancipation Proclamation actually did not free anyone. It only pertained to the areas that had withdrawn from the Union and not then in Union control. It had no effect on the slaves in the border states or areas like Tennessee that were under Union control. Slavery was abolished by the 13th Amendment in December, 1865.

23. The "Good" Samaritan

Andrew Jackson had no vice president. Nobody who succeeded the president had one until after 1967.

24. General Grant

The initials on the horse could not have been General Grant's. He was born Hiram Ulysses Grant and remained so named until a congressman mistakenly make out his appointment to West Point as Ulysses S. Grant. The congressman assumed Ulysses was his first name and Simpson, his mother's maiden name, was his middle name. Grant liked his new name and kept it.

For Further Study:

Grant's early army career was rather rocky, as was his later business career. Persistence and hard work, however, led him upward. Have the class research his early life, Civil War career, presidency, and later years to get a picture of the whole man. His life seemed to be an endless roller coaster of highs and lows, yet he died a hero in the eyes of the American people.

25. The Real Thing

The Confederates usually named battles for the nearest town while the Union named them for the nearest body of water. The official Confederate name for Antietam was Sharpsburg. It is highly unlikely that Stonewall Jackson, writing to another Confederate, would use the Federal name for the battle. The letter needs more careful scrutiny before it could be accepted as authentic.

For Further Study:

Other items to look at in this battle are:

1. Order No. 191: Lee's plan of battle was found by Union troops but they failed to act upon them quickly enough to ensure victory. Why?

2. It was the bloodiest day of the war: 23,500 men fell.

3. Burnsides' Bridge: Repeated charges were made across a narrow stone bridge at frightful cost, when the troops could have waded across. Why?

4. A.P. Hill: A fascinating general, he was on the mind of both Lee and Jackson as they died.

26. Pony Express

Grandpa could not have retired from the Pony Express after 25 years. The company ended after 1½ years when the telegraph replaced it. The promoters were financially ruined.

27. Just Charge It

First of all, Roosevelt was not a general. He was a lieutenant colonel. Command of the group belonged to Colonel Leonard Wood. There was no cavalry charge up San Juan Hill. Most of the regiment's horses were left in Florida. The charge took place on foot. In fact, the regiment came to be known as "Wood's Weary Walkers."

For Further Study:

1. Discuss the role of the press in this war.

2. Discuss the personality of Teddy Roosevelt. Does the fact that they fought on foot detract from their accomplishment?

3. It has been reported that the charge of the Rough Riders, like Bunker Hill, was actually made on another hill. They then joined the battle for San Juan Hill. Have someone research this.

28. In Spirits and in Truth

Mrs. Hayes was known as "Lemonade Lucy" because she would not allow alcohol in the White House for any reason.

29. The Big War

We did not fight it out to the very end with all our allies. Germany signed the armistice on November 11, 1918, ending the war. Russia signed a separate peace with Germany on December 15, 1917, and withdrew her troops then. The Bolsheviks, under Lenin and Trotsky, had overthrown the Kerensky government and decided to make peace with Germany as soon as possible. This was the beginning of communism in Russia.

30. Submarine Sandwich

The *Lusitania* was sunk off the coast of Ireland, not New York.

For Further Study:

1. A study of the history of submarines in other wars would be interesting. The first in the U.S. was the *Turtle*, built in 1776.

2. A discussion of unrestricted submarine warfare could easily turn to rules of war in general. Should we have them at all? Why or why not? Where do new weapons, ones not covered by the rules, fit?

3. Were the Germans justified in pursuing this type of warfare? What reason did they have?

4. Should civilians be able to travel into war zones?

31. Verdun

No American troops were at Verdun. American troops did not arrive in force until 1918.

For Further Study:

1. Why did we enter the war so late? Why at all?

2. Study the use of U.S. troops. At first they were used as replacements in French and English units, much to the displeasure of Pershing. U.S.

troops fought well in several battles under this arrangement and finally got an independent sector. The Argonne Forest was the final great battle for America.

3. Look for other American influence, such as supplies and Wilson's peace plan. Most feel that such influence had a tremendous effect on the German agreement to surrender.

32. A Peace Treaty

Julie: The Treaty of Versailles did not divide Germany into two parts. That was done after World War II.

Charlie: He is wrong in believing that the U.S. signed the treaty. It was never ratified by the U.S. We signed a separate peace treaty in 1921.

For Further Study:

Discuss what effects the treaty had on World War II. What could have been done to prevent it? Can a treaty be made to end all wars? How were the other Central Powers nations handled? Make a treaty that would have been better, yet acceptable to all. How many of Wilson's fourteen points were incorporated into the treaty?

33. Solo Flight

Charles Augustus Lindbergh was born in Detroit, Michigan, not St. Louis, Missouri.

For Further Study:

1. Research Lindbergh's many accomplishments. They include the Congressional Medal of Honor and a Pulitzer Prize.

2. Lindbergh Laws on kidnapping.

3. Why was his plane called *Spirit of St. Louis*? (The people of St. Louis gave money to finance his trip.)

34. A Man with a Plan

Franklin D. Roosevelt had no hard and firm plan of what to do when he was elected president. He knew changes had to be made and gathered the most knowledgeable people he could find to help him decide what to do. He borrowed ideas from the old Progressive party, used lessons learned in World War I concerning cooperation between business and government, and brought in new ideas from his "brain trust" and his Cabinet. He kept what worked and dropped what did not work. The country soon began to move forward again.

For Further Study:

Students could learn a valuable lesson in problem solving from the answer to this mystery. Other areas to investigate are the legislative battles to get Roosevelt's programs passed, the personal charm of the president, and the lasting effects of the New Deal.

Is it possible to have a single policy plan to meet the problems of today's complex world?

35. Crash Landing

Except for Woodrow Wilson's two terms, Republicans had been in office since 1897, and that includes the eight-year period just prior to Hoover's election. Although President Hoover did receive the brunt of the blame for the crash, it was hardly all his fault or the fault of his party. The philosophy of government in those days was to be more an "umpire" instead of a "player" in economics. Depressions had occurred before and the economy had always recovered by itself. This depression was thought to be no different. There were many causes of the Great Depression. Unwise government policies was one, but so were overproduction, stock market speculation and abuses, foreign economic problems, agricultural depression, and the self-generating effects of the depression itself.

For Further Study:

1. Why does the party and president in office get most of the blame or credit for occurrences during their term?
2. What did cause the Great Depression?
3. Why didn't this one correct itself?
4. What prevents a recurrence?

36. Big Ike or Big Mac

It was Operation Overlord, not Torch, that was the allied invasion of Europe. MacArthur did not end the Korean War. He was fired by President Truman in 1951, two years before the war ended.

For Further Study:

1. Look at the other various operations of World War II. Emphasize all the planning that must go into something like this. Each person *must* do his or her part. What if Overlord had failed?

2. Have the students look into the incident of MacArthur's getting fired and the reasons for it. Was Truman justified? Was MacArthur right? What might have been the consequences if MacArthur had had his own way, both militarily and politically?

37. The Vet

Brooks was lying when he spoke of being aboard the *Arizona* on those long voyages during World War II. The *Arizona* was sunk at Pearl Harbor, our very first battle of the war. It still lies partly submerged at the naval base and stands as a memorial for those killed in the Japanese sneak attack on December 7, 1941. More than 1000 men are entombed aboard the *Arizona*.

38. Patton Pending

Mr. Coe was making up the story about landing with Patton on D-Day, and possibly more, too. Patton took no part in D-Day operations, and his Third Army was not formed until after the Normandy landings.

39. Terrible Tarawa

There were no kamikazes at Tarawa. The first one was at Leyte Gulf about one year later.

For Further Study:

1. Look at the mistakes in planning the Tarawa battle. Show how they were used to save countless lives in later landings.

2. Study American tactics and strategy, especially ''island hopping,'' used in World War II.

3. Find the origins of the kamikaze ''Divine Wind'' idea in Japan. Why did they come to use this strategy? Banzai attacks?

4. Would such an idea be acceptable to Americans? (Alamo—is there any connection?)

40. Mr. Truman

The professor suspected that the man was breaking into the library. The "S" in Truman's name does not stand for Simpson or for anything else. His parents named him Harry for his uncle, Harrison Young. They chose the initial "S" but gave him no middle name so that both his grandfathers, Solomon Young and Anderson Shippe Truman, could claim that he had been named in honor of them. Any person who had worked that closely with so much information on Truman would have known that.

41. Kennan's Container

The Grant team made a serious error in saying that the Soviets had no designs on West Berlin. The Berlin Airlift is evidence enough to show that they did. Russia has demanded removal of Western influence several times since then as well.

For Further Study:

1. Study the Berlin Blockade in detail. Everything that was needed for a city of 2,000,000 people was flown in by air. At its height, the airlift was landing one loaded plane in the city every 45 seconds.

2. Study the containment policy to see if it was necessary. Did the Soviets try to take over those nations? What might have been a better policy? Did it cause later tensions?

3. Another topic of interest is the Berlin Wall.

42. Meeting of the Minds

Kennedy was not the youngest president ever to serve. It was Theodore Roosevelt who took office at 42, while Kennedy took office at 43. Kennedy was the youngest "elected" president, though.

43. The Lost Cause

America's failure in Vietnam has been attributed to many causes, but the facts do not support the idea that our troops were any less capable than in any other war.

They won many military victories and often fought very well. Most experts believe that major causes of our failure to achieve a military victory lie beyond the battlefield, in politics and public attitudes toward the war, and in the weaknesses of the South Vietnamese government.

For Further Study:

1. Have the students seek differences between the Vietnam War and our other wars. Look at the military, social, and economic sides of the question.

2. Look for various explanations of the reason for Vietnam's loss. Present the differing views for the class to debate.

3. Have some Vietnam vets address the class, or present an interview with a vet giving the soldier's side of the story.

4. Review the reasons for our involvement there in the first place.

5. Study the peace movement in this country. What effect did it have on the war? Why didn't a peace movement exist in earlier wars?

Note: The Vietnam war is still a highly emotional issue. One should be aware of that fact before making any statements that cannot be supported by hard facts.

44. A Complex Problem

President Nixon did resign, but he was not impeached. The House Judiciary Committee recommended that he be impeached, and adopted three articles of impeachment for consideration by the full House. The articles were for: (1) obstructing justice; (2) abuse of presidential powers; (3) illegally withholding evidence from the judiciary committee. Nixon resigned before the full House of Representatives acted, and President Ford pardoned him of all federal crimes that he might have committed while serving as president.

For Further Study:

1. Tape controversy; right to privacy for the president or other public officials.

2. Presidential pardon—should it have been issued?

3. Congressional attempts to reduce presidential powers during and after Watergate (example: War Powers Resolution).

4. Positive aspects of the Nixon administration.

45. What So Proudly We Hailed

"The Star-Spangled Banner" was written near the end of the War of 1812, not the Revolutionary War. It became popular almost immediately, though not accepted as our national anthem until 1831.

For Further Study:

Music has always been popular in America, and many historical events have given rise to popular songs or become connected to them in some way. Have the students research different eras of history and find the songs that are associated with each. You might want to have them sing the songs or play them in class. Compose a song about the present. What do the songs say about a particular era?

46. Presidential Candidate

No only child has ever been elected president.

Note: This one may be a little hard to find. There are many "presidential trivia"-type books on the market today and the answer can be found in one of those with a little detective work. You may want to give the students this little hint.

47. A Friendly Little Campaign

Dr. Goss has picked out the three principal men involved in one of the most famous elections of all time. The election of 1824 was known as the "Corrupt Bargain" election because it was charged that Clay and Adams conspired to take the presidency away from Jackson. Although most historians feel that nothing sinister did occur, Jackson followers and many citizens felt that the election was stolen. It created much name calling and other less-than-honorable behavior on the part of many supporters of these men. It continued until the 1828 election and even beyond. Dr. Goss probably could not have picked a worse election to use as an example of fair play and honorable behavior.

For Further Study:

1. Unfair attacks have always been a part of American politics. George Washington was deeply hurt and distressed by opposition attacks on him before he left the presidency. It has been much the same for all presidents.

(continued)

Have the students research various elections to see how bad things really got. Of particular interest, besides 1824, is the 1828 election. The 1876 election was also special. Almost all elections in the years from 1824–1900 were full of personal attacks and avoidance of issues.

2. Have students debate whether such tactics are fair, necessary, moral, etc. Why are they used?

3. Follow a current or recent election to see if such attacks occurred. Is there legal recourse for the candidates?

4. Does such behavior occur in foreign countries?

5. Is it human nature to dwell on the negative? What should we do about it?

48. Family Ties

The professor meant that if the nephew does not know any more about history than to believe Teddy and Franklin were father and son, he should have no doubts in appointing Morris to the job. These two Roosevelts were fifth cousins. The only father-son presidents were John Adams and John Quincy Adams. The next most closely related were the Harrisons.

49. Presidential Term Paper

President Gerald Ford was selected as president, not elected for either that office or that of vice president. He was chosen under the Twenty-fifth Amendment as vice president when Spiro Agnew resigned. When Nixon resigned the presidency, Ford moved to that office.

For Further Study:

1. We have had presidents before with limited public-office service—Carter, Reagan, and others. Zachary Taylor was elected in 1848 and had held no civil office nor had he even voted before for any presidential candidate. Have the class study the backgrounds of other presidents and see what experience in public life they have had. What are the positive and negative aspects of such experience?

2. Look for other "informal amendments" in practice in our government. Party nominations for office is one example, as are executive actions like using troops without a declaration of war, executive agreements in lieu of treaties, court decisions, and so on.

3. Make up a problem in which various heads of government have left offices vacant and have the students see who could be in charge.

Note: The part at the end of Sara's paper in which she speculates what would happen if we ever got down to Cabinet-level presidents is just that—speculation. In such a case we would most likely be under dire circumstances and the military would probably be heavily involved. They and the local or state civil authorities would probably be in charge until we could restore the national government. It is interesting food for thought, though.

50. A Better Letter

Writer #3. The Korean War was not a declared war, so his father could not have cast the deciding vote.

For Further Study:

Have the students research their favorite era in history and collect trivia about it. Set aside a class period to let the students ask questions of each other. It should be very interesting and stimulate much research. Maybe you could even create your own trivia game. It also could be used for review before a test.

50A. Who Is Responsible?

Dan is referring to the stated policy of the United States in these matters—to strike militarily only when there is specific evidence that ties a particular act to a particular party. Supporters of that policy believe it places the country on a higher level than any group which strikes blindly at perceived enemies.

For Further Study:

Responses from the students will probably be that we should hit these groups hard and fast. Try to help them see the consequences of such a course of action: (1) We would be seen as a bully nation picking on smaller, weaker countries; (2) any help we might be able to get from moderate groups would disappear; (3) it would probably result in the death of the hostages. Point out that some government critics believe the country has occasionally failed to follow its stated policy—as in the case of the bombing of Libya in 1986.

Questions:

1. When should a military response be used?

2. What can/should we do to ease these tensions?

3. What problems does a free society like ours have in protecting people that a closed society does not have? Which is better?

50B. The Party

It does seem ironic to some people that the most conservative president we have had in years is the one who placed a woman on the Supreme Court, had female and black Cabinet members, and appointed a female U.N. ambassador—all long-time goals of the liberals.

For Further Study:

It should be pointed out to the students that even though Reagan made these breakthroughs, many women and blacks were unhappy. Many women's organizations felt that he did not name enough women to important government positions, and they were angered by his stand on abortion. Many blacks suffered from unemployment and cutbacks in social programs, and this caused them to levy much criticism on Reagan's policies. Many felt that his plans were designed to aid the rich and discriminate against the poor.

A balanced view of his programs is desirable. Have the students study his supply-side theory of economics and let them decide the positives and negatives of it. Can they come up with a better plan? Look into other programs and events of the Reagan presidency: SDI, Grenada, assassination attempt, Iran-Contra affair.

51. Hail Columbia

Columbus sighted America in 1492, not 1429.

52. Live and Let Live

Some settlers came here for religious reasons, but not nearly all of them. They came for many reasons, economic and political as well as religious, and they all did not always get along well with one another.

53. Who's Number One?

The Pilgrim's ship was the *Mayflower*, not the *Nina*.

54. The Incident in Boston

There were no machine guns in 1770.

55. Ben and Bill

He could not know Franklin's brother. The man would have to be at least 200 years old to be still living.

56. Bunker Hill

The British were commanded by General Howe.

57. The Wax Museum

Daniel Boone was not a U.S. president.

58. Georgia Peach

There were no ball-point pens in the 1700s.

59. A Rough Copy

"We the people of the United States" is in the preamble to the U.S. Constitution. There was no United States when the Declaration of Independence was written, so it had to be a fake.

60. United We Stand

The Battle of Yorktown was in Virginia, and that is hardly New England.

61. A College Education

Thomas Jefferson won the 1800 election.

62. Jefferson Papers

Jefferson was long dead by the time of those talks. They were held in the 1920s.

63. Right *Man* for the Job

There has already been a woman on the Supreme Court, Justice Sandra Day O'Connor.

64. A Judicial Review

George is worried about power in the hands of so few. He mentioned that the Court had thirteen members early in the story, but it has only nine, thus putting power in even fewer hands than he thought.

65. A Little Knowledge

The government has three branches, not four. You should explain that we did have limits on our political power, but Americans, even with these restrictions, had far more freedoms and political power than any other people on earth.

66. English Ingenuity

The Industrial Revolution took place in the 18th and 19th centuries, not the 16th century.

67. Old Hickory

Andrew Jackson was dead before the start of the Civil War, so he could not have been wounded in it.

68. New Orleans

The Battle of New Orleans occurred during the War of 1812. It was actually fought after the peace treaty had been signed, but neither side was aware of it at the time.

69. *Old Ironsides*

This ship did not see action in World War I.

70. Captain Ghost

There were no trucks in the Civil War.

71. Thanks But No Thanks

Lincoln was born in Kentucky in a log cabin, not in any Illinois mansion.

72. Mr. Lincoln

The Emancipation Proclamation, not the Gettysburg Address, was what theoretically freed the slaves in areas controlled by the Confederate States.

73. The "Good" Samaritan

Andrew Johnson, not Lyndon, became president after Lincoln. Also, Andrew Johnson had no vice president. Sally knew he was a liar.

74. General Grant

Grant was long dead in 1934.

75. The Real Thing

The Battle of the Bulge took place during World War II, not the Civil War.

76. Pony Express

The Pony Express line began in St. Joseph, Missouri, not New York City.

77. Just Charge It

The group was called the *Rough* Riders, not Range Riders.

78. In Spirits and in Truth

Lucy Hayes refused to serve spirits while in the White House and was known as "Lemonade Lucy" throughout the country. She would not have used the liquor set even if she had owned it.

79. The Big War

Austria was on Germany's side in World War II.

80. Submarine Sandwich

It was the *Lusitania* that was torpedoed, not the *Titanic*. Neither had just left New York, so his whole story was "bologna."

81. Verdun

McClellan did not serve in World War I, and Verdun was fought before America entered the war.

82. A Peace Treaty

The Treaty of Versailles ended World War I, not World War II.

83. Solo Flight

Lindbergh was the first to fly solo nonstop across the Atlantic, not around the world.

84. A Man with a Plan

It was Franklin Roosevelt, not Teddy Roosevelt, who had the New Deal. And the New Deal was not a plan. It was an approach developed as Roosevelt tried to solve the country's problems.

85. Crash Landing

The Great Crash came in 1929, not 1949.

86. Big Ike or Big Mac

1. Ike did not personally lead the troops anywhere, and they were French beaches, not German beaches.

2. MacArthur was never president.

87. The Vet

Brooks did it. The *Constitution* was not in action during World War II.

88. Patton Pending

The Battle of Lookout Mountain occurred during the American Civil War, not World War II.

89. Terrible Tarawa

The *Bismarck* was not at Tarawa. It had been sunk in 1941. At Tarawa it was the U.S. against Japan.

90. Mr. Truman

Professor Micheals suspected that he was a crook. The A-bomb was dropped on Japan, and a man who lived in the museum for ten years should have known that.

91. Kennan's Container

The Grant team stated that Russia was our enemy during World War II. Russia was actually our ally.

92. Meeting of the Minds

President Kennedy was a Catholic, and a teacher of history would surely have known that.

93. The Lost Cause

There were no Chinese troops directly involved in fighting the Vietnam War. The causes of the defeat there were many and complex.

94. A Complex Problem

It was President Nixon who resigned, not Ford.

95. What So Proudly We Hailed

Francis Scott Key wrote "The Star-Spangled Banner." Samuel Clemens was better known as Mark Twain.

96. Presidential Candidate

He could not have served 12 terms in the Senate. Each term there is 6 years. He could not be a Senator until he was 30. That makes him well over 102 years old. He must have meant to say 12 years instead of 12 terms.

97. A Friendly Little Campaign

Washington belonged to no party. They formed later around Alexander Hamilton and Thomas Jefferson.

98. Family Ties

Franklin Delano Roosevelt was much younger than Teddy Roosevelt and could not have been Teddy's father. They were distant relatives though—fifth cousins.

99. Presidential Term Paper

Sara meant the Twenty-fifth Amendment rather than the Thirty-fifth Amendment. We have ratified only twenty-six amendments to date.

100. A Better Letter

General Patton never served in Korea. He was killed in an auto accident just after World War II.

100A. Who Is Responsible?

President Reagan has used military measures several times to resolve such situations. The raid on Libya, the Grenada invasion, and the reflagging of oil tankers in the Persian Gulf are the examples that Dan is about to give him.

100B. The Party

1. The Democrats ran Geraldine Ferraro for vice president in 1984, not 1976.

2. Ronald Reagan appointed Sandra Day O'Connor as our first female Supreme Court justice, appointed female Cabinet members, and a female U.N. ambassador—more women in high positions than any other administration.

American History Mysteries

Student Introduction

Joe Micheals is a professor of history at Central University. Professor Micheals and his graduate assistant, Sally Jones, travel all over the country visiting historical sites, making speeches, and engaging in other activities that involve history in some way.

Each "Mystery" is an account of the various situations and people that Micheals and Jones encounter in their travels. Each story is a mystery in that at least one fact contained in the text is somehow erroneous or misleading. Your job is to carefully read the story and, using logic and historical knowledge, solve the mystery.

Usually, you will not be able to decipher the cryptic statement at the end of the story right away. With a little thought and research, though, you should be able to figure out what's wrong.

Read *carefully* and *think!*

Good Luck.

Note: Be sure to follow your teacher's instructions before writing on your copy.

The names of the non-historical characters that appear in the stories are fictional. Any connection with any real person, living or dead, is purely coincidental.

1. Hail Columbia

"Been in this country long?" asked Professor Micheals.

"We've been here for about two years," replied the man seated across from the professor. "My name is Mr. Nakasoni and this is my son, Ohara."

"Nice to meet you both. I am Professor Joe Micheals and this is my graduate assistant, Sally Jones. We've come to the Nation's Capital to do research on a history book I'm writing."

"That sounds very exciting to me and my son. I am a history buff myself. I was just telling Ohara about your wonderful capital city."

"It certainly does have a colorful past," added Sally.

"Yes," chirped Ohara. "My father has told me that it is in no state, but rather is a territory all to itself."

"That's right," said Sally. "It's called Washington, D.C. The D.C. stands for District of Columbia."

"Yes," said Ohara. "My father says that it's named for the father of your country, George Washington."

"That's correct," smiled the professor. "And do you know where the Columbia part comes from?"

"My father says it's named for Christopher Columbus, the man who first landed on the site in 1492. He was sailing for the country of Spain but was not Spanish. He was really an Italian. My father says that Columbus made four voyages in all to the New World. Queen Isabella and King Ferdinand gave him the money to get the supplies he needed for his voyage, so he claimed vast amounts of territory for them. It must have been terribly exciting for him to make such discoveries."

"Ohara," scolded his father, "do not carry on so about such things. I'm sure these fine people already know all of this about their own country. Besides, here is our stop, so we must go now."

"Sorry you have to go," said Professor Micheals. "I was enjoying the chat. That young man knows a lot about history."

"Thank you, sir," said Ohara, as he rose to leave. "Maybe we'll meet again sometime."

"They certainly were nice," said Sally. "If we do see them again we should straighten them out about Columbus."

"Quite so," said Micheals as he waved good-bye to them. "Quite so."

What were they talking about?

         American History Mysteries

2. Live and Let Live

"Well, it looks as if our plane's going to be delayed quite a while," said the professor. "We might as well try to make the best of it."

"I suppose I'll have time to finish my paper here at the airport instead of on the plane," interjected Mr. Franklin. "Maybe there's some good news today."

"I doubt that!" scowled Mrs. Arnold. "Half the world seems to be trying to kill the other half, and many of them are doing so in the name of religion. It just doesn't make sense to me. Why can't different religious groups learn to get along with one another like we do here in the United States?"

"Yeah!" added Mr. Warren. "We have hundreds of different religious groups in the U.S. and they all seem to tolerate each other fairly well."

"Could be that it's due to our heritage," offered Franklin. "Many of our first settlers came here because of religious persecution."

"That's right," said Mrs. Arnold.

"That's why the Puritans came here. Perhaps they knew how persecution felt and didn't want to hurt others."

"Many religious groups did indeed come here," said Micheals. "We had Anglicans, Jews, Roman Catholics, Lutherans, Quakers, Presbyterians—the list goes on and on."

"If that many different groups could get along well enough to establish a country as great as the United States, then why can't the relatively small number of religious groups that are killing one another get along?" asked Mr. Weathers. "I think they just don't try hard enough. Why can't they learn from our example?"

"It's not a simple problem," said the professor. "Many of these modern-day countries are struggling for political survival, and today's world creates many pressures that our forefathers didn't have to face. Besides that, I would be very careful in using our Colonial period as an example for others to follow in achieving religious toleration."

———————————————————————

What did Professor Micheals mean?

Name: _____   Date: _____

3. Who's Number One?

Professor Micheals was greatly honored at having been selected to chair a round-table discussion on eventual colonization of the moon. He was, however, becoming increasingly concerned about the number of disagreements among the members of the panel, as well as the determination of each member to have his own way.

"As head of the American history department at T.M.I., I feel that I am more than qualified to make a proposal for establishing and maintaining a colony on the moon," said Dr. Robert Terry.

"Of course you are," countered Dr. Ronald Mitchell of Jefferson State, "but don't you agree that the rest of us here have the same right?"

"I have had considerable experience in the field," continued Terry. "More than anyone else here, I'm sure."

"That may be true," said Dr. Margaret Wales of Easton University, "but that doesn't mean that we don't have good ideas, too."

"All I'm trying to say," said Terry, "is that I have done considerable research on the Pilgrims. Being directly involved as I have been in such ventures has sharpened my ideas on colonizing and establishing governments in new areas. My own ancestors landed in Plymouth on the *Mayflower*. I feel that my ties to America's first real permanent settlement gives me the advantage here."

"I'll have you know, sir, that I have ancestors that date back to St. Augustine. A settlement was established there over sixty years before the *Mayflower* got here," said Mitchell.

"I was referring to *English* settlements," snapped Dr. Terry.

"What difference does that make?" asked Dr. Mitchell, his voice rising. "What's the difference between . . . "

"Gentlemen! Gentlemen!" interrupted Dr. Wales. "I think we are forgetting the reason we're all here."

"I quite agree," added Professor Micheals. "And we're forgetting some pretty significant historical facts, too."

What was the professor referring to?

4. The Incident in Boston

"So you're interested in American history," said the young girl seated across from Professor Micheals and Sally Jones.

"That's right, young lady," answered the professor, "and I'm glad to see so many young people interested in the history, too."

"I'm the leader of a youth group traveling around the New England area visiting various historical locations," said Mr. Jackson.

"That's quite commendable of you, sir," said Sally. "I only wish more people were as dedicated to youth as you."

"Quiet now, children! We're about to come to the location of the famous Boston Massacre," spoke Jackson quite excitedly.

"Massacre! How awful!" cried one of the younger group members.

"Don't worry," said Jackson. "It's not as bad as it sounds. On March 5, 1770, Boston was undergoing a very severe winter. A group of residents was just hanging around looking for something to do. Their attention became focused upon a group of British soldiers, who had become quite unpopular as a result of the Quartering Act."

"What was that?" asked a young boy in the group.

"The Quartering Act required that the Colonial government provide for the housing, food, drink, and wages of British soldiers in America. As more and more soldiers arrived here, the cost escalated, and so did resentment among the citizens."

"Why were the soldiers here, Mr. Jackson?" asked Katy.

"The British government said they were needed to protect the Americans, but more and more people began to feel that they were here solely to enforce the unpopular taxes placed on America and to keep the Americans in line. Anyhow, this particular day, a group of citizens began to badger a detachment of British soldiers. For no reason the soldiers opened fire against the unarmed civilians, killing and wounding several."

"How awful!" squealed the children.

"Yes, indeed," said Jackson. "The bus is stopping now. Let's get out and I'll show you just where it happened."

"It is terrible, isn't it," said Micheals as they left the bus.

"Yes it is," said Sally. "But it is a good example of the power of propaganda and semantics."

What did she mean?

5. Ben and Bill

"And how did you enjoy the tour of the Franklin Institute?" asked the cab driver as Professor Micheals entered the cab.

"I found it most enjoyable," replied the professor. "As far as I'm concerned, there's not a more interesting man in all of American history than Benjamin Franklin."

"I'd have to agree with you, sir," said the driver. "There are many things of interest to see here in Philadephia, and many great men have lived and worked here, but Mr. Franklin, in my opinion, was the greatest of all."

"I would like to have spent more time in the Institute, but I was afraid I'd miss my plane."

"I'll have you there in no time, sir. I know what you mean about the Institute, too. Franklin was such a multi-talented person, it's hard to see it all in just one day."

"I'll second that," laughed the professor.

"Just think of all that man did," continued the cabby. "He started the *Pennsylvania Gazette* and wrote *Poor Richard's Almanack*. He established a circulating library, a philosophical society, a fire company, and was postmaster of Philadephia."

"Let's not forget that he also established an academy that later became the University of Pennsylvania," added Micheals.

"Nor his many scientific endeavors," continued the driver. "Of course, his kite-flying episode is well known, and that led to the invention of the lightning rod. The Franklin stove and bifocals were his as well. His interests in science were extensive, and he did work in many varied fields."

"His service to us as a statesman was truly fabulous as well," said the professor. "Among other things, he was a delegate to London before the war as well as a representative in the Continental Congress. He also helped draft the Declaration of Independence and the Constitution."

"It's a little out of our way, sir, but if you wish, I could take you by his first printing office, his home in later life, and his birthplace. It'll cost you a few bucks more, but I'll have you at the airport on time. You can trust me."

"Considering your knowledge about Mr. Franklin, I'm not too sure that I can trust you at all."

What did Professor Micheals mean?

6. Bunker Hill

"Where to, sir?" asked the cabby, as the professor and his graduate assistant Sally Jones got in.

"We're a little early for the conference at Boston University, so why don't you show us some interesting historical sites?" replied Professor Micheals.

"Can do," smiled the cabby, as he pulled away from the airport. "Boston and the surrounding areas are just full of historical sites. Wanna see anything in particular?"

"Well, I'm here to give a speech on the Revolutionary War period. Perhaps something on that subject would be in order."

"Since we're going this way, why don't I show you the site of one of our country's most famous battles?"

"And what would that be?" asked the professor.

"Why, the Battle of Bunker Hill, of course. Everybody's heard of it. Bunker Hill itself is just ahead. Would you like to stop?"

"By all means," said Professor Micheals. "You sound quite knowledgeable on the subject."

"I do like history, but I don't have as much time as I'd like to devote to it."

"Oh, I see," said Micheals, as the three of them walked toward Bunker Hill.

"The British, under Howe and Gage, formed ranks just over there," said the cabby, as they approached the top of Bunker Hill. "Our guys had gotten here first and fortified this hill. When the British advanced, they were repelled several times by William Prescott's men, but the Americans finally had to give up when they ran out of powder and shot. When it was all over, the British had lost over 1000 men and our losses were less than 500 killed and wounded."

"Quite a battle!" said the professor.

"It was a big one, all right. Say, I'd better get back to my cab. You folks like to move on?"

"No, I think we'll look around here for a while," answered Professor Micheals as he paid the fare. "Thanks for the lesson, though. Maybe we'll see you later."

"You're quite welcome," shouted the cabby as he pulled away.

"Nice man," smiled the professor.

"Yes," said Sally. "But isn't it too bad that his historical knowledge doesn't match his enthusiasm."

What did she mean?

7. The Wax Museum

"It certainly was nice of you to give us a personal tour of your museum before the grand opening," said Professor Micheals. "American presidents have always been of keen interest to me."

"Think nothing of it, Professor," said Bill Goddard. "It's an honor for a man of your stature in the field of American history to agree to review my work."

"The likeness of these figures to their photographs is truly remarkable," said the professor. "They seem almost alive."

"It takes years of hard work to be able to make figures of this quality," smiled Goddard. "Our artists are top-quality professionals who take quite a bit of pride in their work. That's why the figures seem so lifelike. We strive for authenticity at all levels of our work."

"Yes, I see," said Micheals. "Even the clothing looks authentic."

"Months and months of research went into this project. We have tried to reproduce everything just as it was. No detail was too small. We tried to cover everything from George Washington's wooden teeth and Jefferson's red hair to Woodrow Wilson's wire-rimmed glasses and Chester A. Arthur's bushy sideburns."

"All that is surely impressive," said the professor, "but if you desire complete authenticity, you must correct at least one mistake."

What mistake was that?

         American History Mysteries

8. Georgia Peach

"I would just love to have some of those fresh juicy peaches," said Sally as they rode along the Georgia countryside. "Let's stop up ahead at that fruit stand and get some."

"That's a great idea, Sally. I love them too."

"Hi y'all," drawled the young Southern woman who worked the stand. "What can I do for y'all?"

"We'd like to stretch our legs a bit and buy some peaches," smiled Micheals. "We've been to Atlanta, attending the history seminar, and we're rather tired."

"Oh, I just love history. My name's Holly. What's yours?"

"I'm Professor Micheals and we're all from Central University."

"What a pleasure to meet y'all," bubbled Holly. "Georgia's just full of history. It was one of the original thirteen colonies, you know."

"Yes, I know," said the professor.

"I have always found it fascinating," Holly continued, "that Georgia has been here longer than the United States has."

"That is something," said Sally as she placed her bag of peaches in front of the young lady.

"History is all over the place in our state," said Holly. "From the Revolution to the Civil War to the world wars, all the way to a president of the United States. Georgia has had a big part in building our country."

"You certainly have a lot to be proud of all right," said the the professor.

"Seems like everywhere you go around here," the girl continued, "there's something of historical value. Everybody is interested in history in this part of the country. The mayor of our little town even claimed to own the pen that Georgia's representative to the First Continental Congress used. It looked just like any old goose feather to me, but he swore it was the original. It made him quite a celebrity for a while."

"What do you mean, for a while?" asked Professor Micheals.

"Well, it seems that his popularity diminished quite a bit after I returned home from college on my summer break. I'm a history major, you see."

What effect would that have on the mayor?

9. A Rough Copy

"I'm sorry," said the professor. "It's just hard for me to believe that a bookstore owner could own such a valuable paper."

"A friend told me that Henry Clark's ancestors and Thomas Jefferson were close friends," said Dr. Dailey. "Jefferson gave his rough draft of the Declaration of Independence to the Clarks as a gift. A financial problem due to family illness is forcing Henry to part with it."

"Let's go have a look at it, then," smiled the professor as he grabbed his coat and hat and started out the door.

"Can I be of service?" asked the owner of Clark's Bookstore.

"Only browsing," smiled Dailey, "but you could show us where your books are on American history."

"Right this way," replied Clark. "Are you professionally involved in history or is it just a hobby?"

"One could safely say that history is a hobby of ours," said Dr. Dailey. "We truly love digging through old books and records."

"Then I must show you my pride and joy. Come on back to my office," said Clark, leading them to the rear of the store.

He stopped in front of an old safe and started turning the dial. He opened the safe and gingerly removed a very old looking sheet of paper with obvious alterations made on the original text.

"Hey, this looks like a copy of Jefferson's first draft of the Declaration of Independence," said Professor Micheals.

"Not exactly," said Mr. Clark. "You see, it's not a copy, but the original. It was given to one of my ancestors by Jefferson himself. My financial situation now forces me to part with it."

"If it is the original, I would be interested," said Dr. Dailey, "but I must be sure that it is the real thing."

"Just listen to these immortal words," replied Clark. "I'll just jump into the text somewhere: 'We hold these truths to be self-evident, that all men are created equal, that they are endowed by their creator with certain unalienable rights, that among these are life, liberty and the pursuit of happiness.' "

"It does look old," said Dr. Dailey, "but I know . . . "

"I would even let you have the paper tested to ascertain the date of its manufacture," interrupted Clark.

"That won't be necessary," said the professor with a smile. "I think Dr. Dailey was trying to say that she wouldn't be interested."

Would she? Why or why not?

10. United We Stand

"This certainly is beautiful country," said the professor, as he and his companion chatted with a group of people in the train's dining car.

"Yes, we like it," replied a crusty old New Englander. "My name's Eb Jacobi and I've lived around here all my life. Where are you from?"

"My name if Professor Joe Micheals, and this is my associate, Professor Mark Christopher. We've come up from Central University to give a series of lectures on the Revolutionary War."

"Well, you're certainly in the right section of the country for that topic," said Jacobi. "Most everyone around here had ancestors who fought in the war. My great-great-great grandfather was a captain under Washington. Yep, there's a lot of interest in the Revolution around here."

"I'm sure there is," added Dr. Christopher. "There's a lot of interest in the birth of our nation in every section of the country."

"That may be, sonny, but most of the real fighting was in this area."

"That's largely true," started Christopher, "but . . . "

"Yep," continued Jacobi, "I've heard stories all my life about the action in this area. Lexington, Concord, Bunker Hill, all tough fights. The British were good, all right, but our boys were better. King George didn't take into consideration the determination of the Americans to see things through when his troops fired on us. The whole country just came together as one to whip the redcoats. They never had a chance, really. The United States was just too much for them."

"Is that so?" smiled the professor.

"Sure enough," laughed Jacobi. "I'd like to chat with you boys some more, but I've got to take care of a little business. Good luck with your talks."

"That just goes to show how time changes things," laughed Professor Micheals.

"No wonder historical accuracy is so hard to maintain," added Christopher.

_____

What were they talking about?

11. A College Education

Professor Joe Micheals and his colleagues, Professor Ronald Wales and Professor Deborah Vaughn, were being interviewed on the topic of the Electoral College. The interviewer, Mr. Grady Reaves, for some reason had taken an adversarial stance with the trio.

"I am neither attacking nor defending this system, Mr. Reaves," said Professor Micheals. "I am simply trying to tell you how and why it was established and what it currently consists of."

"What you implied, sir, was that our founding fathers had too little respect for the judgment of the people of the United States to allow them to elect a president directly!" raved the interviewer.

"You must remember, Mr. Reaves, that we are talking about 1787," added Professor Wales. "Americans were not well educated as a rule then, and news traveled slowly. It would have been utterly impossible for our citizens to cast an informed vote at that time."

"But the mess it created in the 1800 election was terrible," continued Reaves. "I'm amazed it wasn't done away with then."

"That election resulted in the 12th Amendment," interjected Professor Vaughn. "The only major change made was to provide that the electors specify the person voted for as president and the person voted for as vice president."

"Well, I just don't like the whole idea of not voting directly for the person I want for president," continued Reaves. "The whole setup is unnecessary because a president has never been elected who has received fewer votes than his opponent. It would appear from that fact that the American people have pretty good judgment. I simply feel that our electoral college system is outdated and should be replaced. I suppose, though, it would be harder to falsify the 538 votes of the electors, each one knowing who he or she voted for, than it would be to have a computer wrongly credit several thousand nameless votes by the masses to the wrong man."

"Mr. Reaves, you may well be correct on each point you've made," replied Professor Vaughn. "Every point, that is, but one."

Which one?

12. Jefferson Papers

Professor Micheals and his colleague, Dr. Charles D. Christopher, were motoring along the interstate after attending a Civil War conference in Fredricksburg, Virginia. Just outside of Charlottesville they stopped for gas. As was his habit, the good professor became engaged in conversation about local history with a Mr. Roberts, a resident of Charlottesville.

"You know, of course, Professor Micheals, that you are only two miles from Monticello, the home of our great President Thomas Jefferson," said Roberts.

"I did know that we were in the vicinity, but I had no idea we were so close," replied Micheals. "He was truly a great man and a favorite character of mine in history. We must try to find the time to visit his home before we continue on our way."

"Living so close to history certainly has its advantages," smiled Mr. Roberts. "Over the years I have been able to amass a considerable amount of Jefferson collectibles. Since you have a keen interest in him and I am a little short of money, perhaps we could strike a bargain that both of us could be happy with."

"What do you have in mind?" asked Micheals.

"I have in my possession a rather extensive file of original Jefferson papers. One group is incomplete, and due to my limited resources I feel I will never be able to complete the set. I would be willing, therefore, to part with them."

"Original papers are quite valuable," said Micheals. "I am not a rich man, but I believe I could raise funds if the collection is authentic."

"They're the real thing all right," affirmed Roberts. "This particular group is in Jefferson's own hand. It has never been released to the public, however, because it is incomplete. My collection consists of thirty-nine pages of notes Jefferson made while at the Constitutional Convention. He has related his thoughts on government, philosophy, and even on some of the other members in attendance at the Convention. I could let you have it all for only $500. It is really a steal at that price."

"Those papers would be a steal at any price," laughed Dr. Christopher. "You may be short of money, but you certainly aren't short on audacity. Let's go, Joe, I'd like to see some examples of Jefferson's architectural genius."

Why didn't Dr. Christopher think it was a good deal?

13. Right *Man* for the Job

"Joe, I don't think I've ever been more upset," sighed Sally to the professor.

"Whatever do you mean, my dear?" he asked.

"I overheard several of your students voicing their opinions on whether or not a woman was fit to serve on the Supreme Court."

"What's wrong with that?" smiled the professor. "I'm glad they have enough interest in our government to be discussing such relevant topics."

"It isn't their discussing it that's upset me," said Sally. "It's that some people in our country are still so prejudiced about sexual equality."

"Just what, specifically, was said?" inquired Micheals.

"As I said before," replied Sally, "the topic was our Supreme Court. The discussion revolved around women serving as justices on the Court. One student said that it is a shame for us to have any woman on the Court because she could not possibly be qualified to serve. He gave such an impressive presentation of past justices' legal backgrounds and training in legal circles that I'm afraid he may have swayed several students' opinions."

"Could you be a little more specific, Sally?"

"Yes. He spoke of how several men who have served have owned their own law practices or been high-level judges at some state or federal level. He further added that it is virtually impossible for a woman to reach such judicial prominence; therefore, the Constitution's requirement of significant accomplishments in the field of law should bar most women from serving."

"So far he is correct on several points, but what are you so upset about? I realize that it is hard for a woman to climb the ladder of success in some fields, and law could certainly be one, but things are improving."

"I know that it will take time for improvements to be complete," said Sally, "but what bothers me most is that a student as bright as this one obviously is could use the Constitution's requirement for judicial prominence against women in general."

"I wouldn't worry too much about that if I were you, Sally," smiled the professor. "I don't think this young man is as knowledgeable as you give him credit to be."

What does he mean?

17   *American History Mysteries*

14. A Judicial Review

"They're at it again," growled George as he perused his newspaper.

"Who's at it, again, George?" asked the professor from the barber chair.

"Our so-called Supreme Court, that's who," snapped George.

"What have they done now?" asked Fred as he snipped away at the professor's hair. "I thought they were becoming more conservative."

"I thought so, too," snorted George, "but they've just struck down another law, saying it was unconstitutional. I'm sick and tired of that group of nine people telling the whole country what we can do or cannot do. I'm sure it's not supposed to be that way."

"I don't know, George," cautioned Fred. "The Constitution wouldn't have given them the right of judicial review if it didn't want them to have it. There isn't anything we can do about it when it's there in black and white, so why worry about it?"

"We could fire the rascals. That'd show 'em," yelled George. "They'd either have to get in tune with the majority of the people in the country or out they go. Right professor?"

"I'm afraid not," replied Micheals. "Once they become justices, they're there for life unless they resign or do something really wrong."

"You mean we can't get rid of them even when they decide cases against the will of a majority of people in the country?" asked Fred.

"That's right," the professor said. "The setup they have now allows them to make decisions in a way that frees them from pressures of people who might disagree with them. It also lets them look out for the rights of the minority."

"It's still a shame," snarled George. "I thought our founding fathers had more sense than to give such power to a few people."

"Yeah," agreed Fred. "Sometimes the Constitution seems to get in the way more than it helps."

"That may be so in some cases, but I don't think it's directly at fault this time," said Professor Micheals. "Neither are the founding fathers."

What did he mean?

Name: _____ Date: _____

15. A Little Knowledge

Professor Micheals was excited when he received the invitation to chair a discussion on new methods of teaching the U.S. Constitution. The assembled group of high-school government teachers seemed dedicated and anxious to hear his ideas. However, the professor was becoming more and more distressed as one man in the group continually focused on the negative aspects of the document and completely dismissed the positive.

"I just feel that we make too much of this Constitution of ours," continued Mr. Curry. "It did not grant freedom to all our people and I think it should have done so."

"Nobody is claiming that the document is perfect," countered Beau Jones, the leading teacher in the system. "You must understand that, for its time, it set up a form of government that was unique in the world. Americans were given more control over government than any people anywhere."

"If the Constitution was so concerned with the rights of the people," continued Curry, "a bill of rights would have been included from the start, and not added later, as ours was. The founding fathers simply weren't interested in personal liberty, and that cost them much support when ratification time came. All they wanted was to set up a government that would make them rich, or at least keep them from losing any more money."

"But Mr. Curry . . . " started Professor Micheals.

"And, furthermore," interrupted Curry, "if it was so great, why didn't it have the support of more people?"

"What do you mean?" asked Micheals.

"I mean that many prominent American patriots felt they couldn't support it. Patrick Henry was one of these men. Edmund Randolph helped write it but refused to sign it, as did others. All the states were not even represented. If you call that support, then your definition of the word certainly differs from mine."

"Mr. Curry, there is some truth in what you say," said Micheals, "but I'm afraid you don't fully comprehend the overall situation."

"That just goes to show that the old saying about a little knowledge being a dangerous thing is still very true," said Mr. Jones.

What did he mean?

 American History Mysteries

16. English Ingenuity

"We're certainly glad to have you with us, Professor Whitefield," said Sally. "It's not often we get visitors from Oxford to come and speak at our school."

"Glad to be here, my dear. I assure you that I intend to enjoy my visit."

"We'll try to make you feel quite at home, sir," added Professor Micheals. "Is there anything in particular you'd like to see while you're here?"

"I'm very interested in how you Americans are able to achieve such vast industrial output," said Whitefield. "The amount is staggering. If it is possible, I'd like to visit some industrial center."

"I'm sure we could arrange that, sir," said Micheals.

"I distinctly remember, during World War II, how amazed I was by the vast amounts of everything that you produced in such a short time after you became involved in the war. Ships, guns, clothing, food, and airplanes by the thousands. I simple couldn't believe it. I've been fascinated ever since."

"Just good old American ingenuity," laughed Sally.

"I suppose so," chuckled Whitefield, "but you should give us English some of the credit, you know. After all, we're the ones who got your country started. If we hadn't planted colonies here, more than likely you wouldn't be here now."

"That's very true," said Sally. "Other countries had colonies here as well, but I imagine we would be very different from what we are today if not for the English heritage of democratic government."

"Not only in government," continued Whitefield, "but also in industry. If we hadn't freely shared our industrial technology with you in the 18th and 19th centuries, you might not be the industrial power you are now. It all started in the 1700s with Hargreave's spinning jenny. Sir Richard Arkwright invented a machine to turn wool or cotton into yarn and thread. The power loom completed the circle and the Industrial Revolution was in full bloom in England. It made us the richest nation on earth for a while, but you Americans were soon reaping the rewards of our inventiveness."

"A strong case can be made for our earliest factories being copied from England's, but I'm afraid I can't agree with your statements on England's industrial benevolence," said Sally.

What did she mean?

Name: _____   Date: _____

17. Old Hickory

"What a man! What a leader he was!" exclaimed the lady behind the professor as they left the Hermitage.

"He was an extraordinary man indeed," agreed the professor. "Andrew Jackson's presidency brought many changes to the American political system that still linger to this very day."

"Just imagine," continued the stranger. "He was born in a log cabin, his father died just before he was born and he was raised by his poor mother, yet he one day rose to our nation's highest office."

"That say's quite a lot about what kind of country we live in," said Micheals thoughtfully. "You seem to know quite a lot about the man. Are you from here in Tennessee?"

"No sir, I'm not. My name's Joy Schroder and I'm from North Carolina. I once read that General Jackson was born near my home and ever since then he's been sort of a hero of mine. My family and I are on vacation here. I wanted to see the home of the man while we had the opportunity."

"The Hermitage really is something to see," said the professor. "I hope to pick up some artifacts of the Jackson era while I'm here. I like to collect historical objects of all sorts. It's my hobby."

"I have a few collectibles that concern Jackson myself," said the lady. "I bought a small brooch that Mrs. Jackson was supposed to have worn as First Lady in the White House. Considering all that she went through, it means quite a bit to me. A friend who works in the National Archives sold me a copy of a letter written by the doctor who treated the wounds Jackson received in the Revolutionary War. I hope to get more when we get down to the site of the Battle of Horseshoe Bend in Alabama."

"You shouldn't have any trouble finding artifacts there," said the professor, "but . . . "

"From there we plan to go on to New Orleans and see where he gained his most notable military laurels. I guess we'll have to wait, though. There just isn't enought time to do it all this trip."

"Those places should have plenty of souvenirs, but one must be very careful when buying anything reputed to be personal items of famous people. It's always wise to know as much as you can about the subject before you buy, so you won't be fooled again."

What did he mean, "fooled again"?

18. New Orleans

Professor Micheals was greatly honored to have been asked by the New Orleans city fathers to help organize their city's Founders Day celebration, but was unprepared for one member's enthusiasm.

"This town is just overflowing with rich tradition," bragged Mr. Thompson to the gentlemen seated around him.

"It surely does have its share of historical importance, but to say that New Orleans is the U.S. city with the *most* important historical sites is just not fair," replied the professor. "On what do you base that statement?"

"Well, first of all, New Orleans was founded even before there was a United States."

"So were many other cities," replied another at the table. "What does that prove?"

"I can't think of any other city with such a long and colorful history. It was founded by the French, ruled by the Spanish, then sold to the United States by Napoleon. It survived several wars and was the site of important battles more than once. In fact, it was the Battle of New Orleans that decided the War of 1812. That's where Andrew Jackson defeated the British in the battle that won the war."

"Well, sir . . . " started the professor.

"And that's not all," continued Thompson. "This city was fought over during the Civil War and served our country well during World Wars I and II. What other city could claim such a heritage?"

"I must admit that you paint a very interesting picture of your city, but I'm afraid I must take exception to part of your story."

What part?

19. *Old Ironsides*

"Just think of the stories she could tell if only she could talk," said Robye Davis, as she and the professor were having afternoon coffee at a waterfront cafe.

"Yes indeed," smiled the professor. "She's nearly 200 years old. Each man who sailed on her also would have a tale to tell of his own. Would you like to have served aboard her, Robye?"

"Oh yes!" she beamed. "I can't imagine anything more exciting."

"Which of her exploits would you most like to have been on?"

"That's a hard one," said Robye thoughtfully. "Fighting the Barbary pirates must have been a fantastic adventure."

"What about the fight with the *Guerriere?*"

"Of course! I wouldn't want to leave that one out. The trouble is, there are too many adventures to only choose one. Even her construction is extraordinary in that the bolts that held her together were made in Paul Revere's shop."

"Excuse me," said the waiter courteously, "but are you talking about the *Constitution, Old Ironsides?*"

"Yes we are," answered Robye. "Are you interested in her too?"

"As a matter of fact, I am," continued the waiter. "I've just moved here to Boston and I haven't had time to go see the ship yet."

"It's quite a sight to behold," interjected the professor.

"I'm very much interested in this particular ship. I happen to belong to the family who furnished some of the iron for the armor plating along the sides of the ship. That's why this craft holds such attraction for me. I feel that I'm personally involved with this one. I guess that sounds silly to you."

"Oh, not at all," said Micheals, as he and Robye readied themselves to leave. "I often feel as if I am a part of history myself. I guess it's just wishful thinking on my part, though. Anyway, I think you should visit the *Constitution* as soon as possible. I know you'll be very surprised when you see the fine old ship."

"Well?" asked the professor, as they left the cafe.

"Let's hope it's only a minor lapse in memory," smiled Robye as they continued down the street.

What are they talking about?

20. Captain Ghost

Dr. Edward L. Jones, Jr., the noted Civil War expert, entered Professor Micheal's office just in time to hear him say . . .

"Me, go to a seance! Whatever for? You know I don't believe in things like that." The professor was most surprised at his friend Bobby's suggestion. Bobby was well aware of his skepticism in such matters.

"I know you don't believe in them," Bobby said. "That's exactly why I want you to go. Please come too, Dr. Jones. You're the Civil War expert."

"I don't understand," said the professor. "You want me to go because I won't believe what I'm seeing?"

"Yes! No! Let me explain. My friend Larry is a direct descendant of a captain in Stonewall Jackson's command in the Civil War. While cleaning out the attic one day, Larry found several letters from the captain written after the first Battle of Manassas. There's a whole stack of them."

"Now that's what I call exciting," said the professor, his professional curiosity rising. "Do you think he'd let us look at them?"

"I'm sure he will, but that's not the problem. One of the letters mentions that they buried some gold captured from the Yankees during the battle. He gives a description of the hiding place, but it isn't complete. The last page of the letter is

missing. Larry has been paying a medium $50 per visit to get the missing information and she hasn't helped at all. We would like your opinion as to her credibility. With Dr. Jones along with us as well, we should be able to decide rather handily if we're really getting anywhere."

"It could be very interesting indeed," said the professor. "I'd be glad to come along. What about you, Ed?"

"I can't wait," said Jones. "I like nothing better than a mystery, especially one about the War Between the States. Let's go!"

As they drove to the medium's house they discussed various aspects of the battle. They had become quite excited over the whole thing, especially about the possibility of discovering new information in the unpublished letters of a participant in the battle. Although they weren't able to muster much enthusiasm for the possibility of a spiritualist being able to help them, they decided to try to keep an open mind about the whole situation and just take things as they came. When they arrived at their destination, the session was already in progress . . .

"Can you tell us any more about the treasure?" the medium asked, as the table rose and fell. "Your great-great grandson is here with us. He wants to recover the treasure so your sacrifice won't have been made in vain."

(continued)

20. Captain Ghost (*continued*)

"My grandson?" the voice whispered. "Yes, I'm so glad he will reap the benefits of my hard, dangerous work. There were seven of us," the ghostly voice continued, "who found the gold. We got separated from our command going through a woods and surprised a Yank payroll detachment. We were on them before they knew it. As we tied them up, bugles signaled a regroup and we knew General Lee had ordered a counter-attack. We felt we might be captured ourselves and lose the gold, so we decided to hide it until we could turn it over to our superiors. We just never got time to return to the site to reclaim it. None of us survived to the end of the war so our secret died with us." The voice was getting weaker. "We are here together now, though"—the voice was growing ever weaker—"and the gold, the gold, is still by the large oak, just by the . . . " The voice trailed off to an incoherent mumble, then nothing.

"I'm sorry," the medium said exhaustedly. "I just couldn't hold him any longer. Maybe we'll be able to know more the next time."

"I know enough right now!" snapped Dr. Jones. "And what I know will get you arrested. You do have a very entertaining show, though. Too bad it's all fake."

How did he know?

21. Thanks But No Thanks

"May I be of service, sir?" asked the clerk behind the counter.

"Not right now," said Professor Micheals. "We're just looking."

"Take all the time you want, then. That surely is a beautiful little girl you've got there."

"Why, thank you, sir," blushed the professor with pride. "This is my daughter, Ashley. We're headed for the Smithsonian."

"Oh, then you're tourists?" inquired the clerk.

"That's right," said Micheals. "It's our first time to the capital of our nation and we would like to see it all, especially the historical sights."

"Like history, huh?"

"You might say that," smiled the professor.

"Then we've got a section that you simply must look through. The owner of this store is somewhat a history buff himself. He's retired now and travels all over the country. He hardly ever returns without bringing something back either to add to his personal collection or to sell here in the store."

"Sounds great," said the professor. "Let's see what you have."

"Right this way, sir," said the clerk as he led the professor and Ashley to a corner section of the store. "We have a very fine collection of Civil War-era memorabilia. Take, for instance, this fine silver tea service. It came from Robert E. Lee's mansion, Arlington, when Union forces took it over during the war."

"It is beautiful," replied the professor, "but I'm not rich."

"How about something for your daughter then? I'll bet she likes dolls. Here's one that President Buchanan gave to his daughter when he was first elected. It's said to have been her favorite."

"I don't think so," said Micheals.

"Then how about this," continued the clerk. "It's one of General Sherman's bowties. He was hardly every without one, you know, and it's reasonably priced, too. I assure you, sir, that the owner of this store will personally guarantee any merchandise bought in this store to be 100 percent authentic or you'll receive your money back. Would you care to make a purchase now?"

"I don't think so," replied the professor as he turned to leave. "If your employer's integrity is above question then I'm afraid his judgment in buying historical articles isn't."

What did he mean?

22. Mr. Lincoln

"A truly great man," the tour guide was saying as the group stood in front of the Lincoln Memorial. "We all owe this man much. It was he more than any other individual who held this country together during its most trying times."

"He was an amazing man," said the professor to Dr. Linda Cole.

"That's true," said Dr. Cole. "Lincoln's life has always been a pet project of mine. The more I find out about him, the more interesting he becomes."

"I know what you mean," said Micheals. "Even the myths and legends that arise about such men are most fascinating."

"The man who became our 16th president was born in Kentucky on February 12, 1809," the guide continued. "His family moved from Kentucky to Indiana, then later to Illinois."

"This is boring to you, Professor," said Dr. Cole, "but I even like hearing things about him that I've known for years."

"Lincoln was elected to Congress and later was the Republican party's nominee for president. The Republican party had many abolitionists in its ranks, and the South feared that if Lincoln were elected it would mean the end to all that they believed in."

"The guide is quite interesting," noted the professor.

"The first years of the Civil War went badly for the North," continued the guide. "They couldn't seem to find anyone who could defeat the South in a major battle. Lee decided to invade the North and was finally halted at Antietam. This gave Lincoln the chance to do one of the things he is most famous for—the Emancipation Proclamation. This was the document that freed all the slaves in the U.S. forever. This act added many men to the ranks of the North's armies and did the South harm in various ways."

"Interesting as it may be, Professor, I'm sure you'd like to move along," said Dr. Cole. "I know how deeply you resent inaccuracy in any historical subject."

What inaccuracy did she mean?

23. The "Good" Samaritan

"It's very nice of you to stop and offer help," smiled Sally as she looked up at the handsome young stranger. "It's not often that motorists will stop to lend assistance in this day and time."

"That's quite all right," said the motorist as he looked at the engine of Sally's car. "By the way, my name's Roy Perkins."

"I'm Sally Jones. It's nice to meet you. I was on my way to a history class over at the university when my car just died."

"I love history myself," said Roy. "I had an ancestor, on my mother's side, who was vice president of the United States."

"Really!" gasped Sally. "Tell me about it."

"Well, he was a great-great-great uncle of mine. He'd been in politics a long time and was always a staunch Republican. During the Civil War he'd worked his way up to some important committee appointments in the House of Representatives."

"How exciting," said Sally. "Was he Lincoln's running mate?"

"Oh, no," replied Roy, "it was nothing that glamorous."

"What do you mean?" asked Sally.

"After Lincoln's assassination, Andrew Johnson became president. Since Johnson had no vice president," explained Roy, "the Congress approved my uncle to fill the post. My uncle's appointment was quite an honor. The family is still very proud of it."

"Attaining the country's second-highest office is something anyone would be proud of," said Sally coolly.

"I guess so," said Roy, "but all this talk isn't getting your car fixed. Why don't you hop into my car? I'll drop you off at the university so you won't miss class, and I can finish telling you about my uncle on the way."

"No thanks," said Sally. "I've already called my husband from that house across the road and he should be here any minute."

"Sorry I couldn't help," smiled Roy as he headed toward his car. "Good luck!"

As he drove away Roy could see Sally walking toward the house at a brisk pace. "I wonder what gave me away?" he thought.

___

What did?

24. General Grant

"Point Pleasant, Ohio, just five miles ahead. Do you think we'd have time to stop for a few minutes?" asked Dr. Pam Sayre.

"I think we'll make the time," replied the professor. "After all, we might never get the chance to visit General Ulysses S. Grant's hometown again."

As they toured the town, they came to a building with a sign that read *Ulysses S. Grant's Birthplace—Museum and Memorabilia.*

"That looks like the place for us," said Dr. Sayre.

"You're probably right. Let's see what they have to offer."

"Come in," smiled the man at the desk. "If you're interested in General Grant, this is the place to be. My name's Bob Russell."

"I'm Joe Micheals and this is Dr. Pam Sayre. We were just passing through town and thought we'd stop to look around a bit."

"Take all the time you'd like," said Mr. Russell. "Mr. Banks, the museum curator, is on vacation, but I know about all there is to know about the museum here. As you can see, we've got quite a collection. Most of our pieces, though, are from Mr. Grant's early life. Some are even for sale."

"I do collect mementos from time to time," said the professor. "Perhaps, if the price is right, I might find something."

"Well, over here we have one of the saddles that he used during the war. This one was for Cincinnati, his favorite mount."

"I'm sure that's too rich for my blood," said the professor.

"Perhaps a pair of his riding boots from his West Point days?"

"I'm afraid not," said Micheals.

"I have something here that I think will satisfy your needs quite well. The general's love of horses started at an early age and lasted all his life, you know."

"That's right," said Dr. Sayre. "Does that have anything to do with the next item?"

"Quite a bit," said Russell, as he reached into a glass cabinet and pulled out a small wooden horse. "The general carved this horse himself when he was a boy. It's quite authentic. It has the date, June 22, 1834, as well as his initials, U.S.G., carved right into it."

"I guess I'll let that pass, too," said the professor. "Perhaps we'll just look around for a while."

"I wonder if the real curator knows what Mr. Russell is doing?" whispered Dr. Sayre to the professor.

"If he doesn't know now, he will as soon as the Point Pleasant police department informs him of it," replied the professor.

What were they talking about?

25. The Real Thing

Responding to the excited phone call of one of his students, Professor Micheals rushed to the small bookstore on Gordon Street.

"So, where is this letter?" asked the professor. "Let's have a look at it."

"I can hardly wait," said Dr. Ruth Dawson, the world-famous historian and biographer of Thomas Jonathan Jackson. "If the letter is authentic, I'm sure I could use it in my new book."

"I think it was quite a stroke of luck that you happened by my office today," said the professor. "With you along, there should be no question as to whether or not the letter is genuine."

"It's right over here," said Jenny Warren. "I was just looking through this stack of old papers when I ran across the letter. I got so excited when I saw the signature, I just had to call you. It is a letter from General Jackson to his cousin in General Joseph Wheeler's army. It describes a little of the action at the battle of Harper's Ferry and Antietam."

"I see it's dated January 19, 1863," said Dr. Dawson.

"Yes, ma'am," said Jenny. "Right here it tells about General Lee dividing his army in order to capture Harper's Ferry. It says: 'I, with six divisions, was sent to envelop the Federals at Harper's Ferry while Longstreet, with three divisions, moved on Hagerstown.' "

"How exciting!" said the professor.

"The most exciting part, though, is about Antietam," squealed Jenny. "It refers to places like Bloody Lane, the Corn Field, Dunkard Church, and more. It says: 'Just when all seemed lost, A.P. Hill arrived to save the day. His soldiers' blue uniforms helped confuse the Yankees and his crushing flank attack saved our line.' Down toward the end he goes on to say, 'The Battle of Antietam will surely be one of the bloodiest days of the war.' A prophetic statement if ever one was issued. Don't you agree?"

"I sure do," replied Dr. Dawson, "but I'm not sure I can agree that this letter is authentic."

Why?

26. Pony Express

"Yes, sir," bragged the wiry old man as he was ending the group tour of the station, "my great-great grandpa worked this very station for the Pony Express. He started with the company when he was just seventeen. Moved up over the years from rider to manager of this here station. Worked for the Pony Express for twenty-five years, he did."

"Some Pony Express stations were attacked by Indians and the people inside were hurt or killed," said one of the tourists. "Did anything like that happen to your grandpa?"

"Naw, nothing like that," replied the guide. "This post was the beginning of the line that stretched from here in St. Joseph all the way to Sacramento, California. Things were fairly calm at this post compared to some of the other stations down the line."

"Changing horses every fifteen or so miles, dodging Indians, bandits, and bad weather seems to me to be a terribly inefficient method of getting the mail delivered," scoffed one of the group members.

"Not at all," said the professor. "In the 650,000 miles ridden by the Pony Express, the mail was lost only once."

"Are you some kind of Pony Express expert?" asked the scoffer.

"You might say that history is just my hobby," replied the professor genially.

"Not only that," said the guide, "but the postage rate *dropped* from $5.00 a half ounce in the beginning to $1.00. Compare that to your rate changes today."

"It also took only eight to ten days to cover the route," added Micheals. "The overland mail required twelve to fourteen days more. All in all, the Pony Express was rather efficient."

"Well, that's the end of my talk," said the guide. "You all just walk around the grounds and have a look-see. If you have any questions, feel free to ask me."

"Say! Just a minute there," shouted the old man as he hurried to catch up with the professor. "I want to thank you for speaking up for the Pony Express. You helped me out a lot."

"It was my pleasure," said Professor Micheals. "You'd better be a little more careful, though, with what you tell people. You could ruin your credibility by making untrue statements."

***

What was the professor referring to?

27. Just Charge It

Professor Joe Micheals and his good friend Dr. Charlie Bauer were having coffee at a small cafe near campus. They had been discussing Dr. Bauer's new book on the Spanish American War.

"You know, Charlie, I particularly enjoyed the part of your book that dealt with the Rough Riders," said Professor Micheals.

"Teddy Roosevelt has long been a favorite of mine," said Dr. Bauer, "but this is the first in-depth treatment I've ever attempted of his actions in the battle of San Juan Hill."

"Did you say San Juan Hill?" inquired a man at a nearby table.

"Yes we did," answered Dr. Bauer politely.

"I'm sorry to interrupt, but that particular topic is very dear to my heart. Please, let me introduce myself. I'm Joe Williams."

"Well, Mr. Williams, it's always nice to meet a fellow lover of Clio. Won't you join us?" asked the professor.

"Gladly, sirs, but only for a moment. I must leave shortly for an important conference in Washington, D.C. My grandfather was a member of General Roosevelt's original Rough Riders. His name was James Williams, and he was originally a cowboy from Texas. When Mr. Roosevelt started rounding up his regiment, my grandfather heard about it and joined. They soon became fast friends, and my grandfather was given command of a company of troops. He was in the lead the day they charged up San Juan Hill."

"That certainly was a bloody battle," said the professor. "I trust he wasn't hurt."

"Not a scratch," boasted Williams, "but he did have three horses shot out from under him during the famous charge. It's a wonder he wasn't killed. I simply must run, gentlemen. I have several souvenirs of the battle at my home. My favorite one is the set of spurs my grandfather wore during that cavalry charge. There's a Spanish bullet embedded in one of them. Give me a call and I'll show them to you. Good day, sirs."

"That was some story, Charlie."

"You said it! I hope he is better prepared for his Washington conference than he is for a discussion of the Spanish American War."

What did Dr. Bauer mean?

28. In Spirits and in Truth

"It certainly is beautiful," said Sally Jones as she waited for the professor, "but I'm just not sure."

"But wouldn't it be nice to leave this conference on Civil War and Reconstruction with such a valuable collector's item as this?" asked the antique dealer. "Here in Washington everyone knows that Rutherford B. Hayes is the president who withdrew Union forces from the South, thereby helping mend the nation's wounds after the war."

"I am aware of that part," said Sally, "but what does all of that have to do with this serving set?"

"Why, young lady," gasped the shopkeeper in surprise. "Mrs. Hayes was one of the most respected First Ladies of all time, and this is the very set she always used to serve spirits to her guests on important occasions. It was kept in the president's study the whole time he was in office. Just imagine the important people who partook of her hospitality."

"I see," said Sally, "but how can I be sure this set is authentic?"

"Glass can easily be dated, my dear," said the owner. "You have my blessings if you'd like to take the entire set or any piece of it to any shop in town to verify the period in which it was made."

"That won't be necessary," interjected Professor Micheals as he joined the conversation. "If you're that sure of the period, then I'm sure that other dealers would be also."

"Then I would like very much to own the set," said Sally. "Imagine me owning the liquor serving set that Mrs. Hayes used in the White House. I wouldn't have thought it possible."

"It would be quite a feat," laughed Micheals as he escorted Ms. Jones to the door, leaving the complete set behind on the counter.

Why didn't he want her to buy it?

29. The Big War

"You young fellows don't know how it was at all," said the stately-looking old man at the Veterans' Organization's annual meeting. "Back during the big war, World War I of course, we had it much rougher than any other troops in any war. I remember it as if it were yesterday."

"But Mr. Williams," protested Professor Micheals, "I don't see how you can make a statement like that. I was in Korea, and things were pretty unpleasant there."

"I'm sure it was, Professor, but you still didn't have our problems. The Germans were a tough enough foe by themselves, but we also had to contend with poison gas, trench warfare, and totally unheard-of new instruments of war, such as tanks and planes. I remember it right down to the last detail, the whole bloody and awful thing."

"Professor Micheals had to endure bitter cold and screaming Chinese, and you survived all the things you mentioned, Mr. Williams, but what about me?" asked Colonel Hill. "Vietnam was no bowl of cherries. We had steaming hot days, rain that lasted for months, booby traps, and an enemy that could just disappear into the general population any time it wanted. They were kept as well supplied as we were by the Russians and Chinese,

and they were masters at their craft—guerilla warfare. Most of our troops were young and unprepared for that type of fighting. When you add on the red tape and political squabbling we had to put up with, it's a wonder we performed as well as we did."

"Those problems were troublesome indeed, but not insurmountable, Colonel," Williams continued. "One thing missing in your war was large numbers of troops from other nations. Although you had some foreign troops with you there, you still couldn't have had the comradeship we did. I'll never forget fighting right alongside British, French, and even Russian troops. We fought and died side by side and all stuck it out till the very end. That was about the only pleasant aspect of the whole experience."

"I'm sure you have precise recollections, Mr. Williams, of which you should be proud," smiled Professor Micheals, "but for the sake of historical accuracy, I'm afraid I must point out to you your mistake about . . . "

What?

30. Submarine Sandwich

"Mind if I join you folks?" asked the stranger. "It's a little crowded here today and I don't see any other place to sit."

"We don't mind at all," smiled Sally. "Please be seated."

"My name is Joe Micheals and this is Sally Jones," said the professor. "We're in town to catch the conference on World War I."

"Nice to meet you both. I'm Rob Frances. World War I was my war, sonny. If you want to know anything about it, just ask me."

"We were discussing how we entered the war in the first place," said the professor. "I believe the main cause was . . . "

"I'll tell you all about that," interrupted Frances. "It was those darn submarines of Germany's."

"I'd say that they certainly had a major . . ." started Sally.

"Yep!" continued Frances. "Those machines were certainly scary. Nothing like them had ever been used before in warfare."

"The new sub was an awesome weapon, indeed," added Sally, "but actually they had been around for some time."

"Not like these monsters, though," countered Frances. "These things almost won the war single-handedly for Germany. Why, they were sinking more ships than the allies could replace."

"Actually, it was their unrestricted use of . . . "

"You said a mouthful there, young lady. I was on the *Lusitania* when it was torpedoed. Killed nearly 1200 people—civilians—men, women, and children. We sank in just eighteen minutes."

"How did you manage to survive?" asked Sally.

"I was a young man then," answered Frances. "The blast threw me overboard and I clung to debris and paddled my way to shore. Luckily, we had just left New York harbor and were only three or four miles out to sea. I was more fortunate than a lot of folks."

"I must admit," said Micheals, "the sinking of the *Lusitania* did help push us into war with Germany."

"I hope you enjoyed the story, folks, but I see some old friends over in the corner and they're motioning to me to come and eat with them. It's sure been nice talking with you, though."

"He seems like a nice guy," said Sally, "but I hope he doesn't order bologna."

"What do you mean?" asked Micheals.

"Well, it seems to me that he's full enough of that already," she laughed.

What did she mean?

31. Verdun

"You certainly have a beautiful country," said Professor Micheals as he surveyed the scenery from the hillside cafe overlooking the Verdun battlefield. "It's a shame such beauty had to witness such slaughter in World War I."

"Indeed," replied his host, Mr. Jacques Pétain. "It was this battle more than any other than made my grandfather a hero."

"Do you mean that General Henri Pétain was your grandfather?" asked the professor.

"I certainly do," answered Pétain. "The Germans attacked in February, 1916, expecting to crush our forces under the general in a matter of days. Instead, the battle lasted eleven months and ended with the repulse of the enemy."

"Yes, it was a victory for the allies," said Micheals, "but it was at great cost."

"Almost one million were lost here, my friend," said Pétain, the emotion beginning to well in his eyes. "All those men, cut down in the flower of youth. War is a terrible thing, but so is the loss of freedom. So many have died defending it. You Americans know well the sacrifices necessary for being free."

"That we do, Jacques," said Professor Micheals. "We've given much, time after time, to defend our rights."

"And also the rights of others," added Pétain. "We couldn't have won here at Verdun without you. Your General Blackjack Pershing was a superb commander who handled his troops well in battle. American men and materiel might well have been the deciding factor in World War I, and they definitely were in World War II. The world owes you a great debt."

"I deeply appreciate what you've said, Jacques, but I feel that I must correct one little error in our conversation."

What was it?

32. A Peace Treaty

"We seem to have a difference of opinion here," smiled Professor Micheals as he surveyed his American history class. "Mr. Charlie Jackson thinks that the Treaty of Versailles was a good one, and Ms. Julie Ames feels that it was a terrible treaty. Perhaps we should let the two of you present your own viewpoints."

"That's fine with me," said Julie, "because I know what I'm talking about. The treaty divided Germany into two countries, took away all her colonies, and forced her to accept sole war guilt. It further prevented her from being armed while all her enemies had all the munitions they could want. I'd hardly say that a situation like that would help ensure world peace. Germany was stripped of her national pride. No wonder Adolf Hitler had little trouble in rallying the people behind the Nazi party. They were the ones who promised to return Germany to being a nation of strength."

"I hear what you're saying, Julie, but you aren't taking a few things into consideration," countered Charlie. "The territory she lost was transferred chiefly on the basis of nationality. That means that the areas she lost were primarily inhabited by people of another nation anyway, and they simply rejoined their country of origin. Her colonies were turned over to the League of Nations with the goal of their eventually becoming free. Germany was disarmed as a start toward world disarmament—an idea still kicked around today. Furthermore, it created the League of Nations, a forerunner to our United Nations. I think this was a good treaty."

"The main thing it was supposed to do was to keep war from ever happening again," said Julie, "and it certainly failed at that."

"I don't think any treaty, then or now, could guarantee world peace," said Charlie. "The purpose of this treaty was to end World War I, and it did do that rather well. Besides, the United States wouldn't have signed the treaty if it was as bad as you say it is."

"Now hold on," interjected the professor. "This thing is getting a little out of hand. Both of you have made some good points, but both have also made mistakes."

What are they?

33. Solo Flight

"I enjoy St. Louis very much every time I get to come here," said Sally to the professor as they left their plane. "It's a shame we won't be able to go sightseeing this time."

"I know what you mean," said the professor, "but we've got to be back at Central this evening."

As they were going through the airport lobby, Sally noticed a small airplane hanging from the ceiling near the entrance of a souvenir stand.

"What's that?" she asked. "That model plane looks familiar."

"It sure does," replied the professor. "Let's take a look."

"Isn't this a replica of Charles A. Lindbergh's plane, *Spirit of St. Louis?*" Sally asked the man behind the counter.

"Sure is, lady. It's a model of Lindbergh's famous plane named for this very city. We thought it would be an attention-getter for our shop here."

"It got our attention right enough," said Micheals. "What are you selling?"

"Oh, the usual stuff you'd find in any airport gift shop," said the proprietor. "We've also got loads of 'Lucky Lindy' memorabilia. You see, he

was a hero of mine. That's why I call my shop the Lone Eagle Gift Shop. I figure it's the least I could do for the first man to make a nonstop solo flight across the Atlantic."

"Lindy was quite a guy, all right," said Sally.

"He was my inspiration as a young man," continued the shopkeeper. "Being born and raised here I guess I naturally would look up to a man like that. We've got everything a body could want in terms of stuff about the man and his famous flight. I've got a house full of mementos at home."

"It's nice to have a hero," said Micheals, "and even nicer to be able to make a living from him."

"Sure is," said the man. "He's been real good to me all my life. So good in fact that I'm going to buy the house he was born in and make it a museum. It's only a few blocks away and I could sell tickets to it right here. It ought to make a mint."

"The airlines should do quite well, anyway," said Sally.

What did she mean?

34. A Man with a Plan

"Trouble in Lebanon, terrorist attacks everywhere, Americans being kidnapped. Why don't we do something about it? You're the history professor, Joe. You tell us why we have to endure all this abuse just because we are Americans."

The gang down at the barber shop had been discussing world affairs and were glad to see Professor Micheals come in. They didn't always agree with him, but they did like to hear his opinions.

"Leadership," shouted Bob. "Pure and simple, it's leadership."

"What you mean is lack of leadership," added Harry. "We've got to show some decisiveness and determination before people are going to give America the respect it used to have."

"Sure isn't like the old days," said Will.

"What do you mean?" asked the professor.

"Well, I remember the Depression days," continued Will. "That was the worst time America has ever gone through."

"That's a fact," said Bob emphatically, "and it was leadership that got us through. The country was falling apart right before our eyes and old Franklin Delano Roosevelt was the glue that stuck it all together again."

"What was it about Roosevelt that made it possible for him to turn the country around?" asked the professor. "Did he have something that Mr. Hoover lacked?"

"Sure did!" said Harry. "President Roosevelt had a plan. That's what's wrong with the U.S. today. Our foreign policy is too helter-skelter. We don't have a single unified plan to address world problems."

"That's right," added Will. "F.D.R. laid out his 'New Deal' before the American people and we liked what we saw. He identified the problems and developed ways to correct them. Without his plan of attack and his determination to follow it step by step until we recovered, we would possibly still be in a depression."

"He was a great man, all right," sighed Bob, deep in a state of reflection. "If we could just have a man like that in control now."

"I agree with you on most points," said the professor, "but I feel that I must set the record straight on one thing . . . "

_____

What?

35. Crash Landing

As Sally Jones waited patiently in line for her turn to vote she became increasingly interested in the conversation of the two men behind her.

"You're crazy to vote Republican, Jake," said one man to his friend. "I was there in '29 when Mr. Hoover caused the bottom to drop out of the market. I said then that I'd never vote for another Republican and I haven't."

"Now, come on, Bob! You can't believe that the Republicans caused the Great Crash all by themselves."

"I sure can believe it," countered Bob. "I tell you I was there. President Hoover was one of the richest men ever to hold the office of president of the United States. He got in there and didn't do one thing to help the little man in our country and, in fact, let the whole economy flop. My folks lost everything they had."

"I still can't believe that one party, not to mention one man, was responsible for the crash," said Jake. "It just isn't possible."

"Like I said, sonny, I was there. I remember the Hoovervilles and the Hooverbuggies just like it was yesterday. When something like that happens it's pretty clear where to place the blame."

"People can be wrong, you know," said Jake. "Often things aren't as simple as they appear."

"Well, it was pretty clear to me. Things were great in this country up to the time that Hoover and his Republicans took over. Everybody had good jobs and everyone had money to spend. The Democrats did that for us in the years prior to Hoover. It only took him a little more than a year to wreck it all."

"Excuse me, sir," said Sally, "but you say you remember that time well."

"Yes, ma'am, I do," said Bob emphatically. "I remember it all. I was just telling Jake here that I was there. Things had never been so good in the U.S. as they were during the ten or so years before Hoover and his Republicans came to office and ruined it all."

"Well then, sir, if I were going to give the Republicans full blame for the crash, I'd give them a little credit for the good times, too."

What did she mean?

36. Big Ike or Big Mac

"What's the problem here?" Professor Micheals asked the two students arguing outside his door.

"Sorry, Professor," said Ralph, "Jan and I were just discussing generals Eisenhower and MacArthur."

"Come into my office and let's settle this," said Micheals.

"Yes, sir," they answered rather sheepishly as they took a seat in front of the professor's desk.

"Now," said Micheals. "Tell me what this is all about."

"Well, sir," said Jan, "it started as a result of your last lecture. We are approaching World War II in our studies, and Ralph and I began talking about various generals involved in the war."

"That's right," added Ralph. "Jan says that Eisenhower was a greater general than MacArthur, and I took exception to that."

"There were many fine commanders in that war, and it's often very hard to place one as being better than another. You must remember that each one was in a unique position."

"We realize that, sir," continued Jan, "but Dwight Eisenhower rose from the rank of colonel to General of the Army by 1944. He was made Supreme Allied Commander and was in charge of the largest and most crucial undertaking of the war: Operation Torch, the allied invasion of

Europe. After the war he commanded all NATO forces in Europe, then was president of the United States for two terms. MacArthur never had a string of accomplishments like that!"

"He was never president," said Ralph, "but he was a *real* leader. His father won the Congressional Medal of Honor in the Civil War and Mac won one in 1942. He graduated first in his class from the military academy and became a general in World War I. In 1941 he was commander of all U.S. forces in the Far East and bravely defended the Philippines until he was ordered to Australia. He kept his 'I shall return' promise in 1944 when he liberated the islands. He personally received the Japanese surrender and became her postwar administrator. Much credit belongs to him for Japan's remarkable postwar recovery. In Korea he was U.N. commander and won the war for us. He came home to huge crowds and a hero's welcome. Many wanted him to run for president, too, but he declined."

"Both men were truly great Americans and both had great accomplishments," said Micheals. "Instead of fussing about who was greater, why don't each of you research the other general's career and try to discover the mistake that each of you has made today."

What mistakes did he mean?

37. The Vet

"It was too dark for me to see the man clearly," said Professor Micheals, "but I'm sure it's one of these men. The pickpocket went into the crowd at the veterans' meeting, and of all the people in that room only these three were wearing dark-brown pants, the same as the thief."

"I see," said Inspector Holmes. "You didn't see the man who accosted you, but you did notice his clothing."

"That's right," said the professor. "I felt a tug on my wallet, then it was gone. I turned quickly around and saw the back of a man in brown trousers running away from me into the conference room. There was no one else in the vicinity, so it had to be him."

"And what did you do then?" asked Holmes.

"I had just left the meeting and knew there was no other way out. The doors were already chained in preparation to close the building. I merely summoned a guard and had him detain people fitting the description of the thief as they came out. These are the men."

"We certainly are," said Mr. Wilson, one of the men. "I'm late for an appointment and I must be on my way. I was a marine in World War II. I fought on Iwo Jima and Okinawa and I didn't do all that to be harassed by the police for something I didn't do. You'll be hearing from my lawyer if I'm not out of here soon."

"For goodness sake, Wilson," said Mr. Berry, another of the men. "I was at both those places and at Tarawa, too, with the Marines. Your experiences there should have taught you patience."

"That's right," said Mr. Brooks, the third suspect. "You wouldn't be in such a hurry if it were you who had been robbed. I served on the USS *Arizona*, and if I learned anything during those long voyages during the war, it was patience. Why don't you just sit back and take it easy? Unless, of course, you've got something to hide."

"Are you sure it's one of these men?" asked Holmes.

"More sure now than ever. One of these gentlemen just made a mistake that will cost him quite a bit of time. Now where did you stash my wallet, Mr. _____ ?"

_____

Who did it?

38. Patton Pending

"I have always been fascinated by these big machines," commented the professor to his two young nephews as they walked among the lines of tanks at the army museum. "I had many friends who served in them and some who died in them."

"They sure are big," said Daniel. "They're even bigger than a bulldozer."

"Did you ever drive one?" asked Michael hopefully.

"No, I've never had the chance," replied the professor, "but I've always wanted to."

"There's no other experience quite like it," said a stranger who was looking at a big M60 battle tank. "What these babies won't go over or around, they go through. There's no experience in the world like the one you get in a tank. My name's Bill Coe, and I couldn't help but overhear the boy's conversation. Maybe I can help."

"Do you know a lot about tanks?" asked Michael.

"Well, I know something about them," answered Coe. "I drove one for General George Patton in World War II."

"Boy!" shouted Daniel. "Tell us about it!"

"Patton or tanks?" asked Coe.

"Both!" shouted the boys in unison.

"Well, fellows, tanks have been used in war ever since the British used them against the Germans in the Battle of the Somme in 1916. That was during World War I, you know. The first ones were slow and clumsy but they were improved continuously and became a major battlefield weapon. Their destructive capabilities and the psychological effect they had on ground troops gave them tremendous battlefield impact, especially in my war."

"Why are they called tanks?" asked Michael.

"The British called them water tanks while they were being built, in order to conceal their real purpose. Nobody wanted to let the Germans in on the secret before they could be used on the battlefield."

"And the name stuck?" asked Daniel.

"Sure did," smiled Coe. "Some people began to realize how valuable they could be and wrote whole books on how to use them in war. Germany's use of them was a major part of their early successes in World War II. German General Erwin Rommel was an early innovator who was extremely successful with tanks in battle."

(continued)

38. Patton Pending (*continued*)

"George Patton was another innovator, boys," added the professor. "He won one of the first major U.S. victories of the war at El Guettar in North Africa. Is that where you were with him, Mr. Coe?"

"No, I first met him in London. I was one of the tank commanders in his Third Army. We were in England training for the D-Day invasion."

"You mean you landed on Normandy with Patton?" asked Michael, his eyes wide with excitement.

"Sure did, son," smiled Coe as he patted the boy's head. "Patton's Third Army was one of the most famous outfits in the war. Just being a part of it was a thrill I'll remember forever."

"And you were there?" asked Daniel.

"Right from the start," replied Coe proudly. "I hit Omaha Beach on D-Day with the second wave of troops, right behind Patton and his command staff. Thousands and thousands of men were on the beach trying to fight their way inland. I'll never forget that day as long as I live."

"Boy!" sighed Michael and Daniel excitedly.

"General Patton was one of our best fighters," added the professor. "Isn't there a special section on him inside the museum, Mr. Coe?"

"Yes, there is," replied Coe. "The curator is a personal friend of mine. If you'd like, I'll go ask him if he could let us have a closer look at the stuff inside than you'd normally get on the tour. Maybe you could even get inside one of these tanks."

"That'd be great!" shouted the boys.

"Does that include me, too?" asked the professor hopefully.

"Sure it does," called Coe over his shoulder as he headed for the museum front office. "Just wait right there and I'll arrange everything."

"Boy, did we hit it lucky!" cried Michael. "He sure knows his stuff."

"Yeah, I can't wait to get into one of those tanks," yelled Daniel.

"We don't have permission yet," cautioned the professor. "Wishful thinking can sometimes let you down. It usually doesn't do any harm to dream, though. Mr. Coe is a good illustration of that."

What did Professor Micheals mean?

39. Terrible Tarawa

Professor Micheals had just finished delivering his address to the annual meeting of the Veterans of Foreign Wars in Washington, D.C. The meeting was now over and the men were milling about in small groups, renewing old friendships and making conversation. As he was preparing to leave, the professor became interested in a nearby conversation.

"Yeah, you Marines had it tough all right, but not nearly as tough as we had it," said one of the men.

"Is that so?" replied another in the group. "When we hit Tarawa, we had to wade several hundred yards to the beach under heavy fire because you Navy clowns couldn't get us any closer. We lost nearly 1000 men taking that little rock while you boys sat safely aboard your big ol' ships and watched the action."

"It wasn't our fault that you guys had it so tough. We did all we could do. We bombed the place for two months before you guys hit the beach. Then, to top it all off we poured in 15,000 tons of explosives before the first man landed there."

"That may be true," continued the Marine, "but it wasn't enough. The planning for the operation lacked a lot, and we were the ones who had to pay for it."

"We were under fire, too," argued the sailor. "At least you boys had a place to hide on the island. There was no place for us to go on the ships. When one of those Kamikaze planes comes swooping down out of the sky, there's no place for cover. That's what we had to face, so don't give me that stuff about how bad Tarawa was for you poor Marines."

"It's still not the same . . . " The argument continued as the professor headed for his car.

"Did you hear those guys?" asked an old salt as the professor left the building. "I guess it'll never end between the Navy and Marines."

"I guess not," replied Micheals. "There's no sense making it worse than it really was, though."

What did he mean?

40. Mr. Truman

"Independence is really a lovely little town," said Sally as she and the professor approached the Truman Library entrance. "I wouldn't mind living here myself."

"I'm sorry, folks, but we don't open until noon," the man at the door was saying. "I'm just here to straighten up the place a bit. Actually, I'm the caretaker. Billows is the name, and I sleep in back. This is my home, you see."

"It must be quite exciting living in a place such as this," said Sally. "I'll bet you know everything about President Truman."

"As a matter of fact, I do fancy myself as somewhat an expert on his life. I've held this job for ten years. President Harry Simpson Truman was a truly great man. He had to make several of the toughest decisions in the history of our country."

"That he did," said the professor, glancing casually at the truck parked at the side of the library.

"Like what?" inquired Sally, as Mr. Billows eyed the traffic.

"Well, his toughest was probably whether to drop the atomic bomb on Japan to end World War II. That had to be a terrible weight on his shoulders. The firing of General MacArthur in the Korean War was probably the most controversial decision he made. Many people didn't like that at all."

"I'm sure he had good reason, though," said Sally. "What happened to cause it?"

"I'm sorry," smiled Billows rather nervously, "but I must get on with my work. Why don't you come back at noon, and all your questions will be answered."

"Too bad he couldn't have let us in," said Sally. "He was a very interesting man and seemed quite intelligent."

"I agree totally," said Professor Micheals. "He let us in on one thing, though. He hasn't worked here ten years. He's too intelligent to have made a mistake like that. I think we should call the police."

What did Professor Micheals suspect and why?

41. Kennan's Container

Professor Joe Micheals had been invited to help judge a series of debates on American foreign policy matters being held at Elkmont High School. The Elkmont team had defended the point that our policy of containment in the Cold War years was a logical reaction to Soviet expansionism. Debate on this particular topic was winding down.

"Elkmont, you may now make your closing statement," said the professor to the team.

"It is our belief that George F. Kennan's containment doctrine was a logical and successful policy utilized to halt the spread of communism in Europe and elsewhere," said the Elkmont captain. "The Soviets were trying to extend their influence by supporting Communist parties in several countries. Our policy of containment saved Greece and Turkey from communist control when Britain could no longer afford to support them. The Marshall Plan saved war-ravaged Europe from communist control. In only a few years after the initiation of the plan, most European countries were exceeding their prewar output. The economies of these countries thrived, and the communist parties there lost ground steadily. Iran was also on Stalin's hit list, and it took a stiff protest by President Truman to force the Russians to honor their promise to remove troops from the area. Although the allies were unable to reunite Germany in the postwar period, we were able to keep West Germany and West Berlin free. These are just a few of the successes of our containment policy, but we believe that they adequately demonstrate that his policy was a good one."

"Grant High School, you have three minutes for your final rebuttal."

"It is our contention," stated the Grant captain, "that the U.S. policy of containment was unnecessarily harsh and abrasive to the Soviets and that it was a direct cause of later conflicts such as Korea and Vietnam. After all, Russia was our ally during World War II. The policy so eloquently defended by the Elkmont team did nothing but create tension between the Soviets and the United States. Elections were being held in the Western European countries. If the people living there chose to vote for a communistic form of government, it was their right to do so. As for the question of a reunited Germany, we're talking about a country that had started the most devastating war the world had ever known. The Russians had lost 20 million people in that conflict and they had no desire to see the same thing happen again, which was at least feasible if Germany were reunited. As for West Berlin, Russia never had any plans to annex that area. The containment policy only caused friction between two great powers that escalated over the years. The result was reactionary responses on both sides to any trivial

(continued)

41. Kennan's Container (*continued*)

occurrence, which only heightened tensions the world over. The containment policy was not only unnecessary and unwarranted, but had a negative effect that caused worldwide confrontations and problems."

As the judges scored the arguments, one observer in the audience whispered to her friend, "I certainly hope the judges caught that mistake."

What mistake?

42. Meeting of the Minds

The flight out of Chicago had been delayed because of fog, so Professor Micheals decided to relax in the lounge. There he spotted an old colleague, Dr. Alice Wong, seated at a table by the door.

"It's good to see you again, Dr. Wong," smiled Micheals as he clasped his friend's hand. "It's been a long time."

"Too long!" replied Dr. Wong. "I suppose you're still in love with American history?"

"Yes, I guess I'll always be," laughed Micheals. "Have you seen the headlines in today's paper about the Kennedy Papers theft?"

"Isn't it terrible," said Wong. "If they aren't found soon I'm afraid they never will be."

"That would be too bad for posterity," said the gentleman at the next table. "I don't mean to interrupt, but I couldn't help overhearing your conversation. My name is Jacobs, Sam Jacobs. We all seem to share two things in common: a fog delay and a love of history. I've been teaching it now for fifteen years."

"It's good to meet you, Mr. Jacobs," said Micheals. "Come join us."

"Those stolen papers are irreplaceable," continued Jacobs as he took a seat. "They had never been made public, you know. If they're lost, the knowledge and insights contained in them are gone too. President Kennedy was certainly a brilliant man."

"Image all the contributions he might have made had he lived longer," added Dr. Wong. "We'll never know."

"How true," pondered Micheals.

"His accomplishments were many," said Jacobs. "He was a representative as well as a senator, then went on to be our youngest president ever to serve. Before him, there had never been a president who was Catholic. Now all this seems forgotten. It really is a shame. Oh well, things may be looking up. They just announced my flight. I've enjoyed talking with you."

"Seemed like an agreeable man," observed Wong as the man went out the door. "But I wonder what he really does for a living."

_____

How did Dr. Wong know Jacobs wasn't a history teacher?

43. The Lost Cause

"It's truly a shame that so many had to die," said one of the men in the group milling around the Vietnam Veterans' Memorial in Washington, D.C.

Professor Micheals was in the Nation's Capital to visit his friend, Senator Mike Brock.

"It was a tragic war indeed," said the senator. "56,000 dead and over 300,000 wounded."

"And all for nothing," spoke up another visitor to the memorial.

"I would hardly say for nothing," said the professor.

"We learned lessons in that war that should be reminders to us for a long time," added Brock. "The men and women who served in Vietnam were as brave and tireless as any soldiers in any war."

"I guess you're some kind of expert," an elderly bystander sneered sarcastically. "The fact is that we lost. Our country was involved in that conflict from Eisenhower's presidency into Gerald Ford's. We had over half a million men in that little country and dropped hundreds of thousands of tons of explosives on it and we still didn't win. It's as plain as the nose on your face why we failed."

"I'm afraid I'm still in the dark," said Micheals. "Why don't you enlighten me?"

"The truth is that our troops just couldn't hack it. They couldn't win against a ragtag, poorly equipped army of guerillas. It's that simple," said the gentleman matter-of-factly.

"Sometimes, sir, the nose on your face isn't as plain as you might think," said Senator Brock.

What did he mean?

Name: _____   Date: _____

44. A Complex Problem

"Yes, Sally," said Professor Micheals, "this place was the beginning of the end for President Nixon. Once the burglars caught here in the Watergate building were linked to the White House, things began to steadily worsen for the president."

"Hello, folks!" called a guard rather cheerily. "Can I help you?"

"We were just looking around," said Sally. "Is that all right?"

"It sure is. I'll bet you folks are interested in the break-in of the Democratic headquarters."

"Why, yes, we are," said the professor. "How did you know?"

"Oh, we get lots of people around here who are interested in that. By the way, my name's Martha Banks."

"I'm Professor Micheals of Central University, and this is my graduate assistant, Sally Jones."

"Nice to meet you," smiled Banks. "I'm about to make my rounds. If you'd like, you can come along with me. I was working here when it all happened so I know all about the break-in."

Ms. Banks gave the professor and Sally a grand tour of the whole complex. She also provided them with firsthand information, detailing every event that had even the slightest connection to the break-in that occurred on June 17, 1972.

"You certainly have amassed a wealth of knowledge on the Watergate burglary, Officer Banks," said the professor.

"Well, it's kind of nice to work in a place that is a part of history. Just think," said Banks, "one simple burglary and the arrest of five men led eventually to the removal and imprisonment of key White House officials such as Attorney General Mitchell, and finally to the impeachment and resignation of the president himself. I feel that I owe it to myself and to visitors here to know as much as possible about an event as important as that."

"That is a very good attitude to have, Officer, but you must take care to present facts only," cautioned Sally. "Otherwise, you may cause people to have an unrealistic view of our nation's history."

What did she mean?

45. What So Proudly We Hailed

" 'The Star-Spangled Banner' gives me a thrill each time I hear it," said Sally Jones, "and your band played it magnificently, Dr. Barton."

"Of course they did, my dear. I trained them well," replied the band director rather pompously. "We always put forth our best effort for the homecoming game. It's quite important to have a good show for our contributing alumni."

"The music is stimulating enough," agreed Professor Micheals, "but when you consider the historical events that resulted in such a song, we can appreciate it even more."

"I quite agree, Professor. That's why I insist on all my band members fully researching every piece of music we play," said Barton. "I feel that if they understand the circumstances of a song's origin, they will get a better feel for that song and will be able to play it better."

"That's an interesting theory, Dr. . . . " started Sally.

"For instance," continued the band director, "by researching this particular song, the band members should have been filled with a feeling of patriotism. I would hope that while playing they would have a mental image of the song's author, Francis Scott Key, as he was being held prisoner aboard the British ship that was bombing Fort McHenry. If they could envision 'the bombs bursting in air' as our brave defenders valiantly held on to the fort under heavy attack, then I believe that the same admiration and pride felt by Mr. Key will come bursting forth in the music they play—just as it did in the hearts of the boys defending Baltimore. It was that feeling that helped them hold the fort against heavy odds, and a continuation of that feeling that saw them through to the end of that glorious Revolutionary War to which we owe our freedom today. If my band performs with that kind of intensity and pride, we will always be spectacular."

"As I was saying, sir, that's quite a theory, but . . . "

"I appreciate your thoughts on the topic, young lady, but I must go now to arrange the half-time show. I'll see you both later."

"Well, what do you think about that?" wondered Sally aloud.

"I think he'd better let the band do their own research on the songs," replied Professor Micheals, "or we might have a very confused band."

What did he mean?

46. Presidential Candidate

"How is the campaign going, Senator Wilks?" asked Professor Micheals as he entered the room just before the press conference.

"Quite well, thanks," the senator answered. "The press seems to be treating me fairly in every way. Today is another test, though. Sometimes they can change overnight."

"What will your strategy be today?" inquired the professor.

"Well, I thought I'd give the people just a little of my background to start with, then move right into my political opinions."

"That sounds good to me. People like to know about a politician's life and ideals. If they can relate to you in some way, they'll be more willing to listen to you whether they agree with you or not. By the way, what is your background?"

"There isn't all that much to tell," said the senator. "I was born November 11, 1927, in a small town in Ohio. My parents worked hard and sent me to school where I studied to be a lawyer. After that, I became interested in local and state politics and was elected to office. After eight years in state government, I was elected to two terms in the U.S. House of Representatives, then, finally, to the Senate. That's pretty much my story up to now."

"I think it says a lot for you to have achieved so much on your own. So many politicians get into office because of their wealth or the wealth of their family, but you seem to have done it on your own."

"My family has always been behind me. They would have done more, but they aren't rich. If I'd had any brothers or sisters I probably wouldn't have been able to go to college at all, or at least as soon as I did."

"That sure sounds nice, but I wouldn't tell my story in just that way if I were you. Some people put a lot of faith in the odds, and there isn't any reason to make those odds an issue here."

What is the professor talking about?

47. A Friendly Little Campaign

As Professor Micheals and his friends sat in the restaurant waiting for their food to arrive, the conversation turned to politics.

"I just can't believe how ugly our politics has gotten in the recent past," said Dr. Joann Goss.

"Whatever do you mean?" asked Dr. Garry Scroggins.

"I mean these political campaigns," continued Dr. Goss. "It seems that politicians hardly ever focus on the issues anymore."

"That's right," added Micheals, "and I feel it's a shame. It seems to me that there are plenty of issues worthy of debate, but all we seem to get are personal attacks on the candidates."

"Exactly," continued Dr. Goss. "That's what I'm talking about. It's a shame we can't go back to the good old days when politicians were honorable enough to debate issues, and not stoop to spreading rumors and gossip about one another."

"Just how far back would we have to go, Dr. Goss, to reach these good old days?" asked the professor.

"Probably quite a ways," answered Goss. "I'm a medical doctor and you two are historians, so I know you are much better informed than I am in these matters, because you've studied them in detail. I would imagine, though, that in the days of men like Andrew Jackson, John Quincy Adams, and Henry Clay, political campaigns were clean. These men were much too principled to stoop to mudslinging. I'll bet that politics was on too high a level for any type of smear tactics to be used."

"I hope you wouldn't bet too much on that, Dr. Goss," chuckled Scroggins. "You just might be surprised. I am equally sure, though, that you would have a few surprises for me if medicine were today's topic."

What surprise will Dr. Goss get?

48. Family Ties

"Nepotism! There is no denying it this time!" cried Dr. John Morris. "The only reason you are making Harlan Davis the head of the American history department is because he is your nephew."

Professor Micheals was horror-struck. He had stopped in at Grumley College to visit Sam Leighton, an old friend and now president of the college. He had never expected to see a scene such as this taking place in Leighton's office.

"What's bothering you, Morris, is that I know just as much about history as you," said Davis smugly. "I haven't taught history in a few years, but it's like riding a bike—once you have it you always have it."

"That's not true and you know it," shouted Morris. "It is a prime example of your faulty reasoning, though. That is even more reason for you not to head the department."

"Gentlemen! Gentlemen!" shouted Sam Leighton. "This is all getting out of hand. Let's be civilized about this."

"All I want," said Dr. Morris, "is for the best person to head the department. Anything else will hurt the school and I couldn't tolerate that. What you are about to do will cause irreparable damage to this institution."

"Your position is very understandable," said Dr. Leighton, "but what makes you so sure my nephew couldn't handle the job? He's had the best education money could buy. He has worked hard to try to get ahead, and I see nothing wrong with helping him along a little."

"Neither do I," chimed in the would-be department head. "There is nothing wrong with following in my relatives' footsteps. Even presidents have done that. John Quincy Adams was the son of John Adams. Benjamin Harrison's father was a congressman, his grandfather a president, and his great-grandfather a signer of the Declaration of Independence. Teddy Roosevelt was Franklin Delano Roosevelt's father, and Franklin, by the way, has been found to be related to eleven presidents by blood or marriage. I just want to continue my family's tradition."

"You're correct, Dr. Leighton, in your attempt to help your nephew move up the ladder of success, but it shouldn't be done at the expense of our students and our credibility as an institution of higher learning. He simply isn't the most qualified person for the job, as evidenced by . . . "

"That's just sour grapes, Morris, and you know it!" interrupted Davis. "You're just afraid that it won't be you who heads this department."

"*That* isn't true and *you* know it," responded Morris. "I'll even withdraw my name from consideration if you'll do the same thing. I'll do whatever it takes to make sure that this school gets the best qualified head of the department. You may not think that I am the one for the job, but I can prove that Harlan isn't."

(continued)

48. Family Ties (*continued*)

"You can't prove anything, Morris!" screamed Davis. "But you have my permission to try!"

"Just a min . . . " started Morris, but he was interrupted by Sam Leighton.

"My dear friend, Professor Micheals, you have heard all of this. Can you help me decide? I'm a physicist, not a historian, and I need the best man for the job."

"If that's true then you can't appoint your nephew," said Micheals, "judging from what he just said . . . "

"Yes, let's talk about that," shouted Davis. "There aren't many people who would know all those facts. Right, Professor?"

"Well, I don't know many historians who would have put it quite like you did and that's for sure. Dr. Morris, in my opinion, has demonstrated integrity and unselfishness in his regard for the good of this institution. His past accomplishments are ample evidence that he is eminently qualified for the position. And furthermore, Sam, if your nephew's grasp of American history is as accurate in all areas as it is in presidential family lineage, then your decision will be an easy one."

_____

What did he mean?

49. Presidential Term Paper

Professor Micheals sat at the rear of his classroom, listening intently as Sara Allen presented her term paper to the class.

" . . . It is therefore my considered opinion that the founding fathers never intended the vice president to become president in the event of a vacancy in that office. The original Constitution declared that the powers and duties of the office were to pass to the vice president, but no mention was made of the office being transferred. John Tyler, in 1841, set the precedent of the office itself devolving to the vice president. This practice has been followed ever since. In 1967, the Twenty-fifth Amendment officially made this informal amendment a part of the written document."

"Is the vice presidency then vacant, Sara?" asked a student.

"The Twenty-fifth Amendment says, 'Upon a vacancy of the vice presidency, the president will nominate a candidate who will take office upon confirmation by a majority of both houses of Congress.'"

"What if both the presidency and vice presidency are vacant?"

"In a case whereby both the president and vice president have left their offices vacant, the Presidential Succession Act of 1947 would go into effect. The speaker of the House would be first in line to succeed to the presidency, then the president *pro tem* of the Senate. The secretary of state and the other heads of the Cabinet departments come next, in the order in which they were created."

"Then, Sara, it appears that we could possibly have a president who was not elected to any public office," commented a classmate. "I mean, the Cabinet members are appointed by the president and are not elected by the people, yet they are in line for the presidency."

"That is correct," replied Sara. "I really don't feel that there is any need for alarm, though. We've lasted over 200 years and have never had a president who wasn't either elected to that office or the office of vice president. Besides, if we ever got that far down the line of presidential succession, we would undoubtedly be in serious trouble, and other controls of governmental powers would probably be making major decisions."

"Any other questions?" asked the professor. "Then let me say, Sara, that you did an excellent job with your paper. You were obviously well prepared and are quite knowledgeable on the subject. You did make one little mistake, though . . . "

What?

50. A Better Letter

Answering letters from people interested in various aspects of history is one of Professor Micheal's favorite pastimes. His staff handles much of the work load because the professor is so busy with other activities. Today, though, he has time to drop in and see if any really interesting requests have come his way.

"How does the mail look today?" he asks as he enters the workroom.

"Oh, it's mostly the usual," answers Jack Webb, the professor's office manager. "I do have a few that you might be interested in."

"Okay, let's have them," says the professor as he sits down at his desk.

"Here's one from a student in middle school. He's writing a book about the presidents of the United States. He says he has gathered much information, but would like to know who were our tallest, shortest, and heaviest presidents. Also, were any children ever born in the White House?"

"Another is from a young lady who wants your help in securing the war record of her grand-father. It seems that he was in the battles for Guadalcanal and Iwo Jima. She would also like the names of the men who raised the flag on Mt. Suribachi. She thinks he was one of those men, but doesn't know for sure."

"Another writer," continues Jack, "requests information on the Korean War. It seems that his father was a member of Congress at the time the war broke out. He says that the story has been told in his family that his father is the one who cast the deciding vote that declared war on North Korea. He wants a copy of the *Congressional Record* so he can prove the fact to his friends."

"Two of these letters can be handled rather easily through various research methods," says Professor Micheals. "I can send a reply to the other one right now. That writer either had poor history teachers or slept through class too often."

Which request was that?

Name: _____ Date: _____

50A. Who Is Responsible?

"Another American hostage taken in Lebanon. When is all this going to end?" commented Sally as she and several friends sat by the pool.

"I think it's a sad commentary on the state of America's image abroad," added Grady Snyder. "Things like this didn't happen to Americans until lately."

"And what's that supposed to mean?" asked Dan Green, the famous Wall Street broker. "Are you saying we've suddenly gone down the tubes as a world power?"

"What I'm saying is we used to react to such confrontations with a little backbone. We never let anyone push us around," continued Snyder.

"Now wait a minute," said Sally. "We've tried to get our allies involved and to seek diplomatic solutions to all these problems, yet . . . "

"Yet, it isn't working," interrupted Grady. "These Third World countries think we're only a paper tiger, and they're laughing in our face."

"You don't know what you're talking about, Grady," said Dan. "Look at the raid on Libya, the Grenada invasion, the reflagging of oil tankers in the Persian Gulf, and the destruction of Iran's oil rig there. If that's not showing backbone, then you tell me what would be. I think we're doing about all we can for now."

"Yeah, well, we did all that, and what good did it do? Nothing! That's what!"

"So what would *you* suggest, Grady?" asked Sally. "A full-scale invasion of any country that disagrees with us on an issue?"

"I wouldn't go quite that far," answered Grady, "but I'd sure let those people know who they are dealing with."

"Perhaps that's exactly what we are doing," commented Dan quietly.

What did he mean?

50B. The Party

Professor Micheals found himself in the middle of a very interesting discussion. Governor Mary Ellen Morris and Mr. David R. Brown, the Democratic party national chairman, seemed to be at odds over the governor's support of the Republican candidate for president.

"I simply feel, Governor Morris, that the Democratic candidate deserves your support in this crucial contest," said Mr. Brown.

"And I feel differently," answered Governor Morris.

"But the Democratic party has for years been the liberal party. We're the party that tried to change the status quo and get women into more responsible government positions. Now, just when we need your help most, you turn your back on us. That isn't fair."

"I'm not turning my back on the Democratic party, Mr. Brown," replied Governor Morris. "I am simply following my conviction that the better candidate for president of the United States is the Republican candidate."

"But you've heard all the criticism of the Republicans' record on the issues of women's rights under the Reagan presidency, and you're telling me that you will support a man who is dedicated to continuing those policies for the next four years. I just can't believe it," said Brown.

"Sometimes criticism isn't completely justified, Mr. Brown," continued the governor.

"It is justified this time, Governor Morris, and you know it," answered Brown rather excitedly. "It was the Democrats who ran a woman as its vice-presidential candidate against Ronald Reagan and the Republicans in 1984, and it will be the Democrats who'll finally achieve equality for women in this country. You, of all people, should understand how difficult a job that is. That's why I thought we would be able to count on your help. The Republicans haven't made one attempt to achieve sexual equality, yet they get your support. I find that quite ironic."

"What you should understand, Mr. Brown, is that sexual equality is *one* of the issues I find important in this race. There are numerous others as well, and the Republican candidate and I agree on more of those issues than your candidate. Furthermore, I feel that your estimation of gains for women during the Reagan years is seen through partisan eyes. See if you can detect the irony in this: . . . "

What is she going to tell him?

Easy
Stories

51. Hail Columbia

"Been in this country long?" asked Professor Micheals.

"We've been here for about two years," replied the man seated across from the professor. "My name is Mr. Nakasoni and this is my son, Ohara."

"Nice to meet you both. I am Professor Joe Micheals and this is my graduate assistant, Sally Jones. We've come to the Nation's Capital to do research on a history book I'm writing."

"That sounds very exciting to me and my son. I am a history buff myself. I was just telling Ohara about your wonderful capital city."

"It certainly does have a colorful past," added Sally.

"Yes," chirped Ohara. "My father has told me that it is in no state, but rather is a territory all to itself."

"That's right," said Sally. "It's called Washington, D.C. The D.C. stands for District of Columbia."

"Yes," said Ohara. "My father says that its named for the father of your country, George Washington."

"That's correct," smiled the professor. "And do you know where the Columbia part comes from?"

"My father says it's named for Christopher Columbus, the man who discovered the New World in 1429. He was sailing for the country of Spain but was not Spanish. He was really an Italian. My fathers says that Columbus made four voyages in all to the New World. Queen Isabella and King Ferdinand gave him the money to get the supplies he needed for his voyage, so he claimed vast amounts of territory for them. It must have been terribly exciting for him to make such discoveries."

"Ohara," scolded his father, "do not carry on so about such things. I'm sure these fine people already know all of this about their own country. Besides, here is our stop, so we must go now."

"Sorry you have to go," said Professor Micheals. "I was enjoying the chat. That young man knows a lot about history."

"Thank you, sir," said Ohara, as he rose to leave. "Maybe we'll meet again sometime."

"They certainly were nice," said Sally. "If we do see them again we should straighten them out about Columbus."

"Quite so," said Micheals as he waved goodbye to them. "Quite so."

_____

What were they talking about?

52. Live and Let Live

"Well, it looks as if our plane's going to be delayed quite a while," said the professor. "We might as well try to make the best of it."

"I suppose I'll have time to finish my paper here at the airport instead of on the plane," interjected Mr. Franklin. "Maybe there's some good news today."

"I doubt that!" scowled Mrs. Arnold. "Half the world seems to be trying to kill the other half, and many of them are doing so in the name of religion. It just doesn't make sense to me. Why can't different religious groups learn to get along with one another like we do here in the United States?"

"Yeah!" added Mr. Warren. "We have hundreds of different religious groups in the U.S. and they all seem to tolerate each other fairly well."

"Could be that it's due to our heritage," offered Franklin. "All of our settlers came here because of religious persecution."

"That's right," said Mrs. Arnold.

"That's why the Puritans came here. Perhaps they knew how persecution felt and didn't want to hurt others."

"Many religious groups did indeed come here," said Micheals. "We had Anglicans, Jews, Roman Catholics, Lutherans, Quakers, Presbyterians—the list goes on and on."

"If that many different groups could get along well enough to establish a country as great as the United States, then why can't the relatively small number of religious groups that are killing one another get along?" asked Mr. Weathers. "I think they just don't try hard enough. Why can't they learn from our example?"

"It's not a simple problem," said the professor. "Many of these modern-day countries are struggling for political survival, and today's world creates many pressures that our forefathers didn't have to face. Besides that, I would be very careful in using our Colonial period as an example for others to follow in achieving religious toleration."

What did Professor Micheals mean?

53. Who's Number One?

Professor Micheals was greatly honored at having been selected to chair a round-table discussion on eventual colonization of the moon. He was, however, becoming increasingly concerned about the number of disagreements among the members of the panel, as well as the determination of each member to have his own way.

"As head of the American history department at T.M.I., I feel that I am more than qualified to make a proposal for establishing and maintaining a colony on the moon," said Dr. Robert Terry.

"Of course you are," countered Dr. Ronald Mitchell of Jefferson State, "but don't you agree that the rest of us here have the same right?"

"I have had considerable experience in the field," continued Terry. "More than anyone else here, I'm sure."

"That may be true," said Dr. Margaret Wales of Easton University, "but that doesn't mean that we don't have good ideas too."

"All I'm trying to say," said Terry, "is that I have done considerable research on the Pilgrims. I can trace my own ancestors to their ship, the *Nina*. Being directly involved as I've been in such ven-

tures has sharpened my ideas on colonizing and establishing governments in new areas. I feel that my ties to one of America's first real permanent settlements gives me the advantage here."

"I'll have you know, sir, that I have ancestors that date back to St. Augustine. A settlement was established there over sixty years before the Pilgrims' ship got here," said Mitchell.

"I was referring to *English* settlements," snapped Dr. Terry.

"What difference does that make?" asked Dr. Mitchell, his voice rising. "What's the difference between . . . "

"Gentlemen! Gentlemen!" interrupted Dr. Wales. "I think we are forgetting the reason we're all here."

"I quite agree," added Professor Micheals. "And forgetting some pretty significant historical facts, too."

What was the professor referring to?

54. The Incident in Boston

"So you're interested in American history," said the young girl seated across from Professor Micheals and Sally Jones.

"That's right, young lady," answered the professor, "and I'm glad to see so many young people interested in the history, too."

"I'm the leader of a youth group traveling around the New England area visiting various historical locations," said Mr. Jackson.

"That's quite commendable of you, sir," said Sally. "I only wish more people were as dedicated to youth as you."

"Quiet now, children! We're about to come to the location of the famous Boston Massacre," spoke Jackson quite excitedly.

"Massacre! How awful!" cried one of the younger group members.

"Don't worry," said Jackson. "It's not as bad as it sounds. On March 5, 1770, Boston was undergoing a very severe winter. A group of residents was just hanging around looking for something to do. Their attention became focused upon a group of British soldiers, who had become quite unpopular as a result of the Quartering Act."

"What was that?" asked a young boy in the group.

"The Quartering Act required that the Colonial government provide for the housing, food, drink, and wages of British soldiers in America. As more and more soldiers arrived here, the cost escalated, and so did resentment among the citizens."

"Why were the soldiers here, Mr. Jackson?" asked Katy.

"The British government said they were needed to protect the Americans, but more and more people began to feel that they were here solely to enforce the unpopular taxes placed on America and to keep the Americans in line. Anyhow, this particular day, a group of citizens began to badger a detachment of British soldiers. For no reason the soldiers opened fire with machine guns against the unarmed civilians, killing and wounding several."

"How awful!" squealed the children.

"Yes, indeed," said Jackson. "The bus is stopping now. Let's get out and I'll show you just where it happened."

"It is terrible, isn't it," said Micheals, as they left the bus.

"Ridiculous seems more appropriate to me than terrible," said Sally.

What did she mean?

Name: _____   Date: _____

55. Ben and Bill

"And how did you enjoy the tour of the Franklin Institute?" asked the cab driver as Professor Micheals entered the cab.

"I found it most enjoyable," replied the professor. "As far as I'm concerned, there's not a more interesting man in all of American history than Benjamin Franklin."

"I'd have to agree with you, sir," said the driver. "There are many things of interest to see here in Philadephia, and many great men have lived and worked here, but Mr. Franklin, in my opinion, was the greatest of all."

"I would like to have spent more time in the Institute, but I was afraid I'd miss my plane."

"I'll have you there in no time, sir. I know what you mean about the Institute, too. Franklin was such a multi-talented person, it's hard to see it all in just one day."

"I'll second that," laughed the professor.

"Just think of all that man did," continued the cabby. "He started the *Pennsylvania Gazette* and wrote *Poor Richard's Almanack*. He established a circulating library, a philosophical society, a fire company, and was postmaster of Philadelphia."

"Let's not forget that he also established an academy that later became the University of Pennsylvania," added Micheals.

"Nor his many scientific endeavors," continued the driver. "Of course, his kite-flying episode is well known, and that led to the invention of the lightning rod. The Franklin stove and bifocals were his as well. His interests in science were extensive, and he did work in many varied fields."

"His service to us as a statesman was truly fabulous as well," said the professor. "Among other things, he was a delegate to London before the war as well as a representative in the Continental Congress. He also helped draft the Declaration of Independence and the Constitution."

"It's a little out of our way, sir, but if you wish, I could take you by his first printing office. His brother still lives close by and I'll introduce you to him. It'll cost you a few bucks more, but I'll have you at the airport on time. You can trust me."

"Considering your knowledge about Mr. Franklin, I'm not too sure that I can trust you at all."

What did Professor Micheals mean?

56. Bunker Hill

"Where to, sir?" asked the cabby, as the professor and his graduate assistant Sally Jones got in.

"We're a little early for the conference at Boston University, so why don't you show us some interesting historical sites?" replied Professor Micheals.

"Can do," smiled the cabby, as he pulled away from the airport. "Boston and the surrounding areas are just full of historical sites. Wanna see anything in particular?"

"Well, I'm here to give a speech on the Revolutionary War period. Perhaps something on that subject would be in order."

"Since we're going this way, why don't I show you the site of one of our country's most famous battles?"

"And what would that be?" asked the professor.

"Why, the Battle of Bunker Hill, of course. Everybody's heard of it. Bunker Hill itself is just ahead. Would you like to stop?"

"By all means," said Professor Micheals. "You sound quite knowledgeable on the subject."

"I do like history, but I don't have as much time as I'd like to devote to it."

"Oh, I see," said Micheals, as the three of them walked toward Bunker Hill.

"The British, under Lord Cornwallis, formed ranks just over there," said the cabby, as they approached the top of Bunker Hill. "Our guys had gotten here first and fortified Breed's Hill. When the British advanced, they were repelled several times by William Prescott's men, but the Americans finally had to give up when they ran out of powder and shot. When it was all over, the British had lost over 1000 men and our losses were less than 500 killed and wounded."

"Quite a battle!" said the professor.

"It was a big one all right. Say, I'd better get back to my cab. You folks like to move on?"

"No, I think we'll look around here for a while," answered Professor Micheals as he paid the fare. "Thanks for the lesson, though. Maybe we'll see you later."

"You're quite welcome," shouted the cabby as he pulled away.

"Nice man," smiled the professor.

"Yes," said Sally. "But isn't it too bad that his historical knowledge doesn't match his enthusiasm."

What did she mean?

57. The Wax Museum

"It certainly was nice of you to give us a personal tour of your museum before the grand opening," said Professor Micheals. "American presidents have always been of keen interest to me."

"Think nothing of it, Professor," said Bill Goddard. "It's an honor for a man of your stature in the field of American history to agree to review my work."

"The likeness of these figures to their photographs is truly remarkable," said the professor. "They seem almost alive."

"It takes years of hard work to be able to make figures of this quality," smiled Goddard. "Our artists are top-quality professionals who take quite a bit of pride in their work. That's why the figures seem so lifelike. We strive for authenticity at all levels of our work."

"Yes, I see," said Micheals. "Even the clothing looks authentic."

"Months and months of research went into this project. Since we are dealing only with American presidents, we wanted everything just right. No detail is too small. We tried to cover everything from Daniel Boone's coonskin cap and Jefferson's red hair to Woodrow Wilson's wire-rimmed glasses and Chester A. Arthur's bushy sideburns."

"All that is surely impressive," said the professor, "but if you desire complete authenticity, you must correct at least one mistake."

What mistake was that?

American History Mysteries

58. Georgia Peach

"I would just love to have some of those fresh juicy peaches," said Sally as they rode along the Georgia countryside. "Let's stop up ahead at that fruit stand and get some."

"That's a great idea, Sally. I love them too."

"Hi y'all," drawled the young Southern woman who worked the stand. "What can I do for y'all?"

"We'd like to stretch our legs a bit and buy some peaches," smiled Micheals. "We've been to Atlanta, attending the history seminar, and we're rather tired."

"Oh, I just love history. My name's Holly. What's yours?"

"I'm Professor Micheals and we're all from Central University."

"What a pleasure to meet y'all," bubbled Holly. "Georgia's just full of history. It was one of the original thirteen colonies, you know."

"Yes, I know," said the professor.

"I have always found it fascinating," Holly continued, "that Georgia has been here longer than the United States has."

"That is something," said Sally as she placed her bag of peaches in front of the young lady.

"History is all over the place in our state," said Holly. "From the Revolution to the Civil War to the world wars, all the way to a president of the United States. Georgia has had a big part in building our country."

"You certainly have a lot to be proud of all right," said the the professor.

"Seems like everywhere you go around here," the girl continued, "there's something of historical value. Everybody is interested in history in this part of the country. The mayor of our little town even claimed to own the pen that Georgia's representative to the Constitutional Congress used. It looked just like any old ball-point pen to me, but he swore it was the original. It made him quite a celebrity for a while."

"What do you mean, for a while?" asked Professor Micheals.

"Well, it seems that his popularity diminished quite a bit after I returned home from college on my summer break. I'm a history major, you see."

What effect would that have on the mayor?

59. A Rough Copy

"I'm sorry," said the professor. "It's just hard for me to believe that a bookstore owner could own such a valuable paper."

"A friend told me that Henry Clark's ancestors and Thomas Jefferson were close friends," said Dr. Dailey. "Jefferson gave his rough draft of the Declaration of Independence to the Clarks as a gift. A financial problem due to family illness is forcing Henry to part with it."

"Let's go have a look at it, then," smiled the professor as he grabbed his coat and hat and started out the door.

"Can I be of service?" asked the owner of Clark's Bookstore.

"Only browsing," smiled Dailey, "but you could show us where your books are on American history."

"Right this way," replied Clark. "Are you professionally involved in history or is it just a hobby?"

"One could safely say that history is a hobby of ours," said Dr. Dailey. "We truly love digging through old books and records."

"Then I must show you my pride and joy. Come on back to my office," said Clark, leading them to the rear of the store.

He stopped in front of an old safe and started turning the dial. He opened the safe and gingerly removed a very old looking sheet of paper with obvious alterations made on the original text.

"Hey, this looks like a copy of Jefferson's first draft of the Declaration of Independence," said Professor Micheals.

"Not exactly," said Mr. Clark. "You see, it's not a copy, but the original. It was given to one of my ancestors by Jefferson himself. My financial situation now forces me to part with it."

"If it is the original, I would be interested," said Dr. Dailey, "but I must be sure that it is the real thing."

"Just listen to these immortal words," replied Clark. "I'll just jump into the text somewhere: 'We, the people of the United States, hold these truths to be self-evident, that all men are created equal, that they are endowed by their creator with certain unalienable rights, that among these are life, liberty and the pursuit of happiness.'"

"It does look old," said Dr. Dailey, "but I know . . ."

"I would even let you have the paper tested to ascertain the date of its manufacture," interrupted Clark.

"That won't be necessary," said the professor with a smile. "I think Dr. Dailey was trying to say that she wouldn't be interested."

Would she? Why or why not?

60. United We Stand

"This certainly is beautiful country," said the professor, as he and his companion chatted with a group of people in the train's dining car.

"Yes, we like it," replied a crusty old New Englander. "My name's Eb Jacobi and I've lived around here all my life. Where are you from?"

"My name is Professor Joe Micheals, and this is my associate, Professor Mark Christopher. We've come up from Central University to give a series of lectures on the Revolutionary War."

"Well, you're certainly in the right section of the country for that topic," said Jacobi. "Most everyone around here had ancestors who fought in the war. My great-great-great grandfather was a captain under Washington. Yep, there's a lot of interest in the Revolution around here."

"I'm sure there is," added Dr. Christopher. "There's a lot of interest in the birth of our nation in every section of the country."

"That may be, sonny, but most of the real fighting was in this area."

"That's largely true," started Christopher, "but . . . "

"Yep," continued Jacobi, "I've heard stories all my life about the action in this area. Yorktown, Lexington, Concord, Bunker Hill, all tough fights. The British were good, all right, but our boys were better. King George didn't take into consideration the determination of the Americans to see things through when his troops fired on us. The United States was just too much for them."

"Is that so?" smiled the professor.

"Sure enough," laughed Jacobi. "I'd like to chat with you boys some more, but I've got to take care of a little business. Good luck with your talks."

"That just goes to show how time changes things," laughed Professor Micheals.

"No wonder historical accuracy is so hard to maintain," added Christopher.

What were they talking about?

61. A College Education

Professor Joe Micheals and his colleagues, Professor Ronald Wales and Professor Deborah Vaughn, were being interviewed on the topic of the Electoral College. The interviewer, Mr. Grady Reaves, for some reason had taken an adversarial stance with the trio.

"I am neither attacking nor defending this system, Mr. Reaves," said Professor Micheals. "I am simply trying to tell you how and why it was established and what it currently consists of."

"What you implied, sir, was that our founding fathers had too little respect for the judgment of the people of the United States to allow them to elect a president directly!" raved the interviewer.

"You must remember, Mr. Reaves, that we are talking about 1787," added Professor Wales. "Americans were not well educated as a rule then, and news traveled slowly. It would have been utterly impossible for our citizens to cast an informed vote at that time."

"But the mess it created in the 1800 election was terrible," continued Reaves. "Abe Lincoln had to be elected president by the Congress."

"That election resulted in the 12th Amendment," interjected Professor Vaughn. "The only major change made was to provide that the electors specify the person voted for as president and the person voted for as vice president."

"Well, I just don't like the whole idea of not voting directly for the person I want for president," continued Reaves. "The whole setup is unnecessary. I simply feel that our electoral college system is outdated and should be replaced. I supposed, though, it would be harder to falsify the 538 votes of the electors, each one knowing who he or she voted for, than it would be to have a computer wrongly credit several thousand nameless votes by the masses to the wrong man."

"Mr. Reaves, you may well be correct on each point you've made," replied Professor Vaughn. "Every point, that is, but one."

_____

Which one?

62. Jefferson Papers

Professor Micheals and his colleague, Dr. Charles D. Christopher, were motoring along the interstate after attending a Civil War conference in Fredricksburg, Virginia. Just outside of Charlottesville they stopped for gas. As was his habit, the good professor became engaged in conversation about local history with a Mr. Roberts, a resident of Charlottesville.

"You know, of course, Professor Micheals, that you are only two miles from Monticello, the home of our great President Thomas Jefferson," said Roberts.

"I did know that we were in the vicinity, but I had no idea we were so close," replied Micheals. "He was truly a great man and a favorite character of mine in history. We must try to find the time to visit his home before we continue on our way."

"Living so close to history certainly has its advantages," smiled Mr. Roberts. "Over the years I have been able to amass a considerable amount of Jefferson collectibles. Since you have a keen interest in him and I am a little short of money, perhaps we could strike a bargain that both of us could be happy with."

"What do you have in mind?" asked Micheals.

"I have in my possession a rather extensive file of original Jefferson papers. One group is incomplete, and due to my limited resources I feel I will never be able to complete the set. I would be willing, therefore, to part with them."

"Original papers are quite valuable," said Micheals. "I am not a rich man, but I believe I could raise funds if the collection is authentic."

"They're the real thing all right," affirmed Roberts. "This particular group is in Jefferson's own hand. It has never been released to the public, however, because it is incomplete. My collection consists of thirty-nine pages of notes Jefferson made while at the League of Nations. He has related his thoughts on government, philosophy, and even on some of the other members in attendance at the Conferences. I could let you have it all for only $500. It is really a steal at that price."

"Those papers would be a steal at any price," laughed Dr. Christopher. "You may be short of money, but you certainly aren't short on audacity. Let's go, Joe, I'd like to see some examples of Jefferson's architectural genius."

Why didn't Dr. Christopher think it was a good deal?

63. Right *Man* for the Job

"Joe, I don't think I've ever been more upset," sighed Sally to the professor.

"Whatever do you mean, my dear?" he asked.

"I overheard several of your students voicing their opinions on whether or not a woman was fit to serve on the Supreme Court."

"What's wrong with that?" smiled the professor. "I'm glad they have enough interest in our government to be discussing such relevant topics."

"It isn't their discussing it that's upset me," said Sally. "It's that some people in our country are still so prejudiced about sexual equality."

"Just what, specifically, was said?" inquired Micheals.

"As I said before," replied Sally, "the topic was our Supreme Court. The discussion revolved around women serving as justices on the Court. One student said that it is a shame for us to have any woman on the Court because she could not possibly be qualified to serve. He gave such an impressive presentation of past justices' legal backgrounds and training in legal circles that I'm afraid he may have swayed several students' opinions."

"Could you be a little more specific, Sally?"

"Yes. He spoke of how several men who have served have owned their own law practices or been high-level judges at some state or federal level. He further added that it is virtually impossible for a woman to reach such judicial prominence. That's why no woman has ever served on the Supreme Court or ever will."

"So far he is correct on several points, but what are you so upset about? I realize that it is hard for a woman to climb the ladder of success in some fields, and law could certainly be one, but things are improving."

"I know that it will take time for improvements to be complete," said Sally, "but what bothers me most is that a student as bright as this one obviously is could sway opinions about women in general."

"I wouldn't worry too much about that if I were you, Sally," smiled the professor. "I don't think this young man is as knowledgeable as you give him credit to be."

What does he mean?

64. A Judicial Review

"They're at it again," growled George as he perused his newspaper.

"Who's at it, again, George?" asked the professor from the barber chair.

"Our so-called Supreme Court, that's who," snapped George.

"What have they done now?" asked Fred as he snipped away at the professor's hair. "I thought they were becoming more conservative."

"I thought so, too," snorted George, "but they've just struck down another law, saying it was unconstitutional. I'm sick and tired of that group of thirteen people telling the whole country what we can or cannot do. I'm sure it's not supposed to be that way."

"I don't know, George," cautioned Fred. "They wouldn't have the right of judicial review if it wasn't a good idea. There isn't anything we can do about it, so why worry about it?" said Fred.

"We could fire the rascals. That'd show 'em," yelled George. "They'd either have to get in tune with the majority of the people in the country or out they go. Right professor?"

"I'm afraid not," replied Micheals. "Once they become justices, they're there for life unless they resign or do something really wrong."

"You mean we can't get rid of them even when they decide cases against the will of a majority of people in the country?" asked Fred.

"That's right," the professor said. "The setup they have now allows them to make decisions in a way that frees them from pressures of people who might disagree with them. It also lets them look out for the rights of the minority."

"It's still a shame," snarled George. "I thought our founding fathers had more sense than to give such power to a few people."

"Yeah," agreed Fred. "But the problem you're talking about is actually worse than you think."

What did he mean?

65. A Little Knowledge

Professor Micheals was excited when he received the invitation to chair a discussion on new methods of teaching the U.S. Constitution. The assembled group of high-school government teachers seemed dedicated and anxious to hear his ideas. However, the professor was becoming more and more distressed as one man in the group continually focused on the negative aspects of the document and dismissed completely the positive.

"I just feel that we make too much of this Constitution of ours," continued Mr. Curry. "It did not grant freedom to all our people and I think it should have done so."

"Nobody is claiming that the document is perfect," countered Beau Jones, the leading teacher in the system. "You must understand that, for its time, it set up a form of government that was unique in the world. Americans were given more control over government than any people anywhere."

"But it kept control from the people," continued Curry. "It set up four branches of government, with only the House of Representatives being elected directly by the people. That's only 25% of our government."

"But Mr. Curry . . . " started Professor Micheals.

"And, furthermore," interrupted Curry, "if it was so great, why didn't it have the support of more people?"

"What do you mean?" asked Micheals.

"I mean that many prominent American patriots felt they couldn't support it. Patrick Henry was one of these men. Edmund Randolph helped write it but refused to sign it, as did others. All the states were not even represented. If you call that support, then your definition of the word certainly differs from mine."

"Mr. Curry, there is some truth in what you say," said Micheals, "but I'm afraid you don't fully comprehend the overall situation."

"And furthermore," said Mr. Jones, "you're just plain wrong on one point."

What did he mean?

66. English Ingenuity

"We're certainly glad to have you with us, Professor Whitefield," said Sally. "It's not often we get visitors from Oxford to come and speak at our school."

"Glad to be here, my dear. I assure you that I intend to enjoy my visit."

"We'll try to make you feel quite at home, sir," added Professor Micheals. "Is there anything in particular you'd like to see while you're here?"

"I'm very much interested in how you Americans are able to achieve such vast industrial output," said Whitefield. "The amount is staggering. If it is possible, I'd like to visit some industrial center."

"I'm sure we could arrange that, sir," said Micheals.

"I distinctly remember, during World War II, how amazed I was by the vast amounts of everything that you produced in such a short time after you became involved in the war. Ships, guns, clothing, food, and airplanes by the thousands. I simple couldn't believe it. I've been fascinated ever since."

"Just good old American ingenuity," laughed Sally.

"I suppose so," chuckled Whitefield, "but you should give us English some of the credit, you know. After all, we're the ones who got your country started. If we hadn't planted colonies here, more than likely you wouldn't be here now."

"That's very true, said Sally. "Other countries had colonies here as well, but I imagine we would be very different from what we are today if not for the English heritage of democratic government."

"Not only in government," continued Whitefield, "but also in industry. If we hadn't freely shared our industrial technology with you during the Industrial Revolution that took place in the 16th century, you might not be the industrial power you are now. It all started with Hargreave's spinning jenny. Sir Richard Arkwright invented a machine to turn wool or cotton into yarn and thread. The power loom completed the circle and the Industrial Revolution was in full bloom in England. It made us the richest nation on earth for a while, but you Americans were soon reaping the rewards of our inventiveness."

"A strong case can be made for our earliest factories being copied from England's, but I'm afraid I must disagree with you on one point," said Sally.

What did she mean?

67. Old Hickory

"What a man! What a leader he was!" exclaimed the lady behind the professor as they left the Hermitage.

"He was an extraordinary man indeed," agreed the professor. "Andrew Jackson's presidency brought many changes to the American political system that still linger to this very day."

"Just imagine," continued the stranger. "He was born in a log cabin, his father died just before he was born and he was raised by his poor mother, yet he one day rose to our nation's highest office."

"That say's quite a lot about what kind of country we live in," said Micheals thoughtfully. "You seem to know quite a lot about the man. Are you from here in Tennessee?"

"No sir, I'm not. My name's Joy Schroder and I'm from North Carolina. I once read that General Jackson was born near my home, and ever since then he's been sort of a hero of mine. My family and I are on vacation here. I wanted to see the home of the man while we had the opportunity."

"The Hermitage really is something to see," said the professor. "I hope to pick up some artifacts of the Jackson era while I'm here. I like to collect historical objects of all sorts. It's my hobby."

"I have a few collectibles that concern Jackson myself," said the lady. "I bought a small brooch that Mrs Jackson was supposed to have worn. Considering all that she went through, it means quite a bit to me. A friend who works in the National Archives sold me a copy of a letter written by the doctor who treated the wounds Jackson received in the Civil War. I hope to get more artifacts when we get down to the site of the Battle of Horseshoe Bend in Alabama."

"You shouldn't have any trouble finding artifacts there," said the professor, "but . . . "

"From there we plan to go on to New Orleans and see where he gained his most notable military laurels. I guess we'll have to wait, though. There just isn't enought time to do it all this trip."

"Those places should have plenty of souvenirs, but one must be very careful when buying anything reputed to relate to famous people. It's always wise to know as much as you can about the subject before you buy, so you won't be fooled again."

What did he mean, "fooled again"?

68. New Orleans

Professor Micheals was greatly honored to have been asked by the New Orleans city fathers to help organize their city's Founders Day celebration, but was unprepared for one member's enthusiasm.

"This town is just overflowing with rich tradition," bragged Mr. Thompson to the gentlemen seated around him.

"It surely does have its share of historical importance, but to say that New Orleans is the U.S. city with the *most* important historical sites is just not fair," replied the professor. "On what do you base that statement?"

"Well, first of all, New Orleans was founded even before there was a United States."

"So were many other cities," replied another at the table. "What does that prove?"

"I can't think of any other city with such a long and colorful history. It was founded by the French, ruled by the Spanish, then sold to the United States by Napoleon. It survived several wars and was the site of important battles more than once. In fact, it was the Battle of New Orleans that decided the Revolutionary War. That's where Andrew Jackson defeated the British in the battle that won the war."

"Well, sir . . . " started the professor.

"And that's not all," continued Thompson. "This city was fought over during the Civil War and served our country well during World Wars I and II. What other city could claim such a heritage?"

"I must admit that you paint a very interesting picture of your city, but I'm afraid I must take exception to part of your story."

What part?

69. Old Ironsides

"Just think of the stories she could tell if only she could talk," said Robye Davis, as she and the professor were having afternoon coffee at a waterfront cafe.

"Yes indeed," smiled the professor. "She's nearly 200 years old. Each man who sailed on her also would have a tale to tell of his own. Would you like to have served aboard her, Robye?"

"Oh yes!" she beamed. "I can't imagine anything more exciting."

"Which of her exploits would you most like to have been on?"

"That's a hard one," said Robye thoughtfully. "Fighting the Barbary pirates must have been a fantastic adventure."

"What about the fight with the *Guerriere?*"

"Of course! I wouldn't want to leave that one out. The trouble is, there are too many adventures to only choose one. Even her construction is extraordinary in that the bolts that held her together were made in Paul Revere's shop."

"Excuse me," said the waiter courteously, "but are you talking about the *Constitution, Old Ironsides?*"

"Yes we are," answered Robye. "Are you interested in her too?"

"As a matter of fact, I am," continued the waiter. "I've just moved here to Boston and I haven't had time to go see the ship yet."

"It's quite a sight to behold," interjected the professor.

"I'm very much interested in this particular ship. You see, my grandfather was seriously wounded while serving aboard her in World War I. That's why this craft holds such attraction for me. I feel that I'm personally involved with this one. I guess that sounds silly to you."

"Oh, not at all," said Micheals, as he and Robye readied themselves to leave. "I often feel as if I am a part of history myself. I guess it's just wishful thinking on my part, though. Anyway, I think you should visit the *Constitution* as soon as possible. I know you'll be very surprised when you see the fine old ship."

"Well?" asked the professor, as they left the cafe.

"Let's hope it's only a minor lapse in memory," smiled Robye as they continued down the street.

What are they talking about?

 American History Mysteries

70. Captain Ghost

Dr. Edward L. Jones, Jr., the noted Civil War expert, entered Professor Micheal's office just in time to hear him say . . .

"Me, go to a seance! Whatever for? I don't believe in them."

"I know you don't," said Bobby, one of the professor's associates. "That's why I want you to go."

"I don't understand," said the professor. "You want me to go because I won't believe what I'm seeing?"

"Yes! No! Let me explain. My friend Larry is a direct descendant of a captain in Stonewall Jackson's command in the Civil War. While cleaning out the attic one day, Larry found some letters from the captain written after the first Battle of Manassas."

"Now that's what I call exciting," said the professor.

"One of the letters tells how they buried some gold captured from the Yankees during the battle. He gives a description of the hiding place, but it isn't complete. Larry has been paying a medium $50 per visit to get the missing information and she hasn't helped a bit."

"It could be very interesting indeed," said the professor. "I'd be glad to come along. What about you, Ed?"

"You bet," said Jones. "I like nothing better than a mystery, especially one about the War Between the States. Let's go!"

"Can you tell us more about the treasure?" the medium asked as the table rose and fell. "Your great-great grandson is here."

"My grandson?" the voice whispered. "Yes, I'm so glad he will reap the benefits of my hard, dangerous work. There were seven of us who found the gold. We surprised a Yank payroll detachment. As we tied them up, bugles signaled a regroup and we knew the general had ordered a counterattack. We felt we might be captured ourselves, so we hid the money in a bombed-out truck on the side of the road and returned to our outfit. None of us survived to the end of the war, so our secret died with us." The voice was getting weaker. "We are here together now, though, and the gold, the gold, is still by the large oak, just by the . . ." The voice trailed off to nothing.

"I'm sorry," the medium said exhaustedly. "I just couldn't hold him any longer. Maybe we'll learn more the next time."

"I know enought right now!" snapped Dr. Jones. "And what I know will get you arrested. You do have a very entertaining show, though. Too bad it's all fake."

How did he know?

71. Thanks But No Thanks

"May I be of service, sir?" asked the clerk behind the counter.

"Not right now," said Professor Micheals. "We're just looking."

"Take all the time you want, then. That surely is a beautiful little girl you've got there."

"Why, thank you, sir," blushed the professor with pride. "This is my daughter, Ashley. We're headed for the Smithsonian."

"Oh, then you're tourists?" inquired the clerk.

"That's right," said Micheals. "It's our first time to the capital of our nation and we would like to see it all, especially the historical sights."

"Like history, huh?"

"You might say that," smiled the professor.

"Then we've got a section that you simply must look through. The owner of this store is somewhat a history buff himself. He's retired now and travels all over the country. He hardly ever returns without bringing something back either to add to his personal collection or to sell here in the store."

"Sounds great," said the professor. "Let's see what you have."

"Right this way, sir," said the clerk as he led the professor and Ashley to a corner section of the store. "We have a very fine collection of Civil War-era memorabilia. Take, for instance, this fine silver tea service. It came from Robert E. Lee's mansion, Arlington, when Union forces took it over during the war."

"It is beautiful," replied the professor, "but I'm not rich."

"How about something from the Illinois mansion that President Lincoln was born in? We just happen to have the gold-plated door knocker from that house."

"I don't think so," said Micheals.

"Then how about this," continued the clerk. "It's one of General Sherman's bowties. He was hardly ever without one, you know, and it's reasonably priced, too. I assure you, sir, that the owner of this store will personally guarantee any merchandise bought in this store to be 100 percent authentic or you'll receive your money back. Would you care to make a purchase now?"

"I don't think so," replied the professor as he turned to leave. "If your employer's integrity is above question then I'm afraid his judgment in buying historical articles isn't."

What did he mean?

72. Mr. Lincoln

"A truly great man," the tour guide was saying as the group stood in front of the Lincoln Memorial. "We all owe this man much. It was he more than any other individual who held this country together during its most trying times."

"He was an amazing man," said the professor to Dr. Linda Cole.

"That's true," said Dr. Cole. "Lincoln's life has always been a pet project of mine. The more I find out about him, the more interesting he becomes."

"I know what you mean," said Micheals. "Even the myths and legends that arise about such men are most fascinating."

"The man who became our 16th president was born in Kentucky on February 12, 1809," the guide continued. "His family moved from Kentucky to Indiana, then later to Illinois."

"This is boring to you, Professor," said Dr. Cole, "but I even like hearing things about him that I've known for years."

"Lincoln was elected to Congress and later was the Republican party's nominee for presi-dent. The Republican party had many abolitionists in its ranks, and the South feared that if Lincoln were elected it would mean the end to all that they believed in."

"The guide is quite interesting," noted the professor.

"The first years of the Civil War went badly for the North," continued the guide. "They couldn't seem to find anyone who could defeat the South in a major battle. Lee decided to invade the North and was finally halted at Antietam. This gave Lincoln the chance to do one of the things he is most famous for—the Gettysburg Address. This was the document that freed the slaves. This act added many men to the ranks of the North's armies and did the South harm in various ways."

"Interesting as it may be, Professor, I'm sure you'd like to move along," said Dr. Cole. "I know how deeply you resent inaccuracy in any historical subject."

What inaccuracy did she mean?

73. The "Good" Samaritan

"It's very nice of you to stop and offer help," smiled Sally as she looked up at the handsome young stranger. "It's not often that motorists will stop to lend assistance in this day and time."

"That's quite all right," said the motorist as he looked at the engine of Sally's car. "By the way, my name's Roy Perkins."

"I'm Sally Jones. It's nice to meet you. I was on my way to a history class over at the university when my car just died."

"I love history myself," said Roy. "I had an ancestor, on my mother's side, who was vice president of the United States."

"Really!" gasped Sally. "Tell me about it."

"Well, he was a great-great-great uncle of mine. He'd been in politics a long time and was always a staunch Republican. During the Civil War he'd worked his way up to some important committee appointments in the House of Representatives."

"How exciting," said Sally. "Was he Lincoln's running mate?"

"Oh, no," replied Roy, "it was nothing that glamorous."

"What do you mean?" asked Sally.

"After Lincoln's assassination, Lyndon Johnson became president. Since Johnson had no vice president," explained Roy, "he chose my uncle to fill the post."

"Attaining the country's second-highest office is something anyone would be proud of," said Sally coolly.

"I guess so," said Roy, "but all this talk isn't getting your car fixed. Why don't you hop into my car? I'll drop you off at the university so you won't miss class, and I can finish telling you about my uncle on the way."

"No thanks," said Sally. "I've already called my husband from that house across the road and he should be here any minute."

"Sorry I couldn't help," smiled Roy as he headed toward his car. "Good luck!"

As he drove away Roy could see Sally walking toward the house at a brisk pace. "I wonder what gave me away?" he thought.

What did?

74. General Grant

"Point Pleasant, Ohio, just five miles ahead. Do you think we'd have time to stop for a few minutes?" asked Dr. Pam Sayre.

"I think we'll make the time," replied the professor. "After all, we might never get the chance to visit General Ulysses S. Grant's hometown again."

As they toured the town, they came to a building with a sign that read *Ulysses S. Grant's Birthplace—Museum and Memorabilia.*

"That looks like the place for us," said Dr. Sayre.

"You're probably right. Let's see what they have to offer."

"Come in," smiled the man at the desk. "If you're interested in General Grant, this is the place to be. My name's Bob Russell."

"I'm Joe Micheals and this is Dr. Pam Sayre. We were just passing through town and thought we'd stop to look around a bit."

"Take all the time you'd like," said Mr. Russell. "Mr. Banks, the museum curator, is on vacation, but I know about all there is to know about the museum here. As you can see, we've got quite a collection. Most of our pieces, though, are from Mr. Grant's early life. Some are even for sale."

"I do collect mementos from time to time," said the professor. "Perhaps, if the price is right, I might find something."

"Well, over here we have one of the saddles that he used during the war. This one was for Cincinnati, his favorite mount."

"I'm sure that's too rich for my blood," said the professor.

"Perhaps a pair of his riding boots from his West Point days?"

"I'm afraid not," said Micheals.

"I have something here that I think will satisfy your needs quite well. The general's love of horses started at an early age and lasted all his life, you know."

"That's right," said Dr. Sayre. "Does that have anything to do with the next item?"

"Quite a bit," said Russell, as he reached into a glass cabinet and pulled out a small wooden horse. "The general carved this horse himself when he was a boy. It's quite authentic. It has the date, June 22, 1934, as well as his initials carved right into it."

"I guess I'll let that pass, too," said the professor. "Perhaps we'll just look around for a while."

"I wonder if the real curator knows what Mr. Russell is doing?" whispered Dr. Sayre to the professor.

"If he doesn't know now, he will as soon as the Point Pleasant police department informs him of it," replied the professor.

What were they talking about?

75. The Real Thing

Responding to the excited phone call of one of his students, Professor Micheals rushed to the small bookstore on Gordon Street.

"So, where is this letter?" asked the professor. "Let's have a look at it."

"I can hardly wait," said Dr. Ruth Dawson, the world-famous historian and biographer of Thomas Jonathan Jackson. "If the letter is authentic, I'm sure I could use it in my new book."

"I think it was quite a stroke of luck that you happened by my office today," said the professor. "With you along, there should be no question as to whether or not the letter is genuine."

"It's right over here," said Jenny Warren. "I was just looking through this stack of old papers when I ran across the letter. I got so excited when I saw the signature, I just had to call you. It is a letter from General Jackson to his cousin in General Joseph Wheeler's army."

"I see it's dated January 19, 1863," said Dr. Dawson.

"Yes, ma'am," said Jenny. "Right here it tells about General Lee dividing his army in order to capture Harper's Ferry. It says: 'I, with six divisions, was sent to envelop the Federals at Harper's Ferry while Longstreet, with three divisions, moved on Hagerstown.' "

"How exciting!" said the professor.

"The most exciting part, though, is about Antietam," squealed Jenny. "It refers to places like Bloody Lane, the Corn Field, Dunkard Church, and more. It says: 'Just when all seemed lost, A.P. Hill arrived to save the day. His soldiers' blue uniforms helped confuse the Yankees and his crushing flank attack saved our line.' Down toward the end he goes on to say, 'The Battle of the Bulge will surely be one of the bloodiest days of the war.' A prophetic statement if ever one was issued. Don't you agree?"

"I sure do," replied Dr. Dawson, "but I'm not sure I can agree that this letter is authentic."

Why?

76. Pony Express

"Yes, sir," bragged the wiry old man as he was ending the group tour of the station, "my great-great grandpa worked this very station for the Pony Express. He started with the company when he was just seventeen. Moved up from rider to manager of this here station."

"Some Pony Express stations were attacked by Indians and the people inside were hurt or killed," said one of the tourists. "Did anything like that happen to your grandpa?"

"Naw, nothing like that," replied the guide. "This post was the beginning of the line that stretched from New York City all the way to Sacramento, California. Things were fairly calm at this post compared to some of the other stations down the line."

"Changing horses every fifteen or so miles and dodging Indians, bandits, and bad weather seems to me to be a terribly inefficient method of getting the mail delivered," scoffed one of the group members.

"Not at all," said the professor. "In the 650,000 miles ridden by the Pony Express, the mail was lost only once."

"Are you some kind of Pony Express expert?" asked the scoffer.

"You might say that history is just my hobby," replied the professor genially.

"Not only that," said the guide, "but the postage rate *dropped* from $5.00 a half ounce in the beginning to $1.00. Compare that to your rate changes today."

"It also took only eight to ten days to cover the route," added Micheals. "The overland mail required twelve to fourteen days more. All in all, the Pony Express was rather efficient."

"Well, that's the end of my talk," said the guide. "You all just walk around the grounds and have a look-see. If you have any questions, feel free to ask me."

"Say! Just a minute there," shouted the old man as he hurried to catch up with the professor. "I want to thank you for speaking up for the Pony Express. You helped me out a lot."

"It was my pleasure," said Professor Micheals. "You'd better be a little more careful, though, with what you tell people. You could ruin your credibility by making untrue statements."

What was the professor referring to?

77. Just Charge It

Professor Joe Micheals and his good friend Dr. Charlie Bauer were having coffee at a small cafe near campus. They had been discussing Dr. Bauer's new book on the Spanish American War.

"You know, Charlie, I particularly enjoyed the part of your book that dealt with Mr. Roosevelt," said Professor Micheals.

"Teddy Roosevelt has long been a favorite of mine," said Dr. Bauer, "but this is the first in-depth treatment I've ever attempted of his actions in the battle of San Juan Hill."

"Did you say San Juan Hill?" inquired a man at a nearby table.

"Yes we did," answered Dr. Bauer politely.

"I'm sorry to interrupt, but that particular topic is very dear to my heart. Please, let me introduce myself. I'm Joe Williams."

"Well, Mr. Williams, it's always nice to meet a fellow lover of Clio. Won't you join us?" asked the professor.

"Gladly, sirs, but only for a moment. I must leave shortly for an important conference in Washington, D.C. My grandfather was a member of General Roosevelt's original Range Riders. His name was James Williams, and he was originally a cowboy from Texas. When Mr. Roosevelt started rounding up his regiment, my grandfather heard about it and joined. They soon became fast friends, and my grandfather was given command of a company of troops. He was in the lead the day they charged up San Juan Hill."

"That certainly was a bloody battle," said the professor. "I trust he wasn't hurt."

"Not a scratch," boasted Williams, "but it's a wonder he wasn't killed. I simply must run, gentlemen. I have several souvenirs of the battle at my home. My favorite one is a set of spurs my grandfather wore during a cavalry charge. There's a Spanish bullet embedded in one of them. Give me a call and I'll show them to you. Good day, sirs."

"That was some story, Charlie."

"You said it! I hope he is better prepared for his Washington conference than he is for a discussion of the Spanish American War."

What did Dr. Bauer mean?

78. In Spirits and in Truth

"It certainly is beautiful," said Sally Jones as she waited for the professor, "but I'm just not sure."

"But wouldn't it be nice to leave this conference on Civil War and Reconstruction with such a valuable collector's item as this?" asked the antique dealer. "Here in Washington everyone knows that Rutherford B. Hayes is the president who withdrew Union forces from the South, thereby helping mend the nation's wounds after the war."

"I am aware of that part," said Sally, "but what does all of that have to do with this serving set?"

"Why, young lady," gasped the shopkeeper in surprise. "Mrs. Hayes was one of the most respected First Ladies of all time, and this is the very set she always used to serve spirits to her guests on important occasions. It was kept in the president's study the whole time he was in office. Just imagine the important people who partook of her hospitality."

"I see," said Sally, "but how can I be sure this set is authentic?"

"Glass can easily be dated, my dear," said the owner. "You have my blessings if you'd like to take the entire set or any piece of it to any shop in town to verify the period in which it was made."

"That won't be necessary," interjected Professor Micheals as he joined the conversation. "If you're that sure of the period, then I'm sure that other dealers would be also."

"Then I would like very much to own the set," said Sally. "Imagine me owning the liquor serving set that Mrs. Hayes used in the White House. I wouldn't have thought it possible."

"It would be quite a feat," laughed Micheals as he escorted Ms. Jones to the door, leaving the complete set behind on the counter.

Why didn't he want her to buy it?

79. The Big War

"You young fellows don't know how it was at all," said the stately-looking old man at the Veterans' Organization's annual meeting. "Back during the big war, World War I of course, we had it much rougher than any other troops in any war. I remember it as if it were yesterday."

"But Mr. Williams," protested Professor Micheals, "I don't see how you can make a statement like that. I was in Korea, and things were pretty unpleasant there."

"I'm sure it was, Professor, but you still didn't have our problems. The Germans were a tough enough foe by themselves, but we also had to contend with poison gas, trench warfare, and totally unheard-of new instruments of war, such as tanks and planes. I remember it right down to the last detail, the whole bloody and awful thing."

"Professor Micheals had to endure bitter cold and screaming Chinese, and you survived all the things you mentioned, Mr. Williams, but what about me?" asked Colonel Hill. "Vietnam was no bowl of cherries. We had steaming hot days, rain that lasted for months, booby traps, and an enemy that could just disappear into the general population any time it wanted. They were kept as well supplied as we were by the Russians

and Chinese, and they were masters at their craft—guerilla warfare. Most of our troops were young and unprepared for that type of fighting. When you add on the red tape and political squabbling we had to put up with, it's a wonder we performed as well as we did."

"Those problems were troublesome indeed, but not insurmountable, Colonel," Williams continued. "One thing missing in your war was large numbers of troops from other nations. Although you had some foreign troops with you there, you still couldn't have had the comradeship we did. I'll never forget fighting right alongside British, French, and Austrian troops. We fought and died side by side and all stuck together. That was about the only pleasant aspect of the whole experience."

"I'm sure you have precise recollections, Mr. Williams, of which you should be proud," smiled Professor Micheals, "but for the sake of historical accuracy, I'm afraid I must point out to you your mistake about . . . "

_____

What?

80. Submarine Sandwich

"Mind if I join you folks?" asked the stranger. "It's a little crowded here today and I don't see any other place to sit."

"We don't mind at all," smiled Sally. "Please be seated."

"My name is Joe Micheals and this is Sally Jones," said the professor. "We're in town to catch the conference on World War I."

"Nice to meet you both. I'm Rob Frances. World War I was my war, sonny. If you want to know anything about it, just ask me."

"We were discussing how we entered the war in the first place," said the professor. "I believe the main cause was . . . "

"I'll tell you all about that," interrupted Frances. "It was those darn submarines of Germany's."

"I'd say that they certainly had a major . . . " started Sally.

"Yep!" continued Frances. "Those machines were certainly scary. Nothing like them had ever been used before in warfare."

"The new sub was an awesome weapon, indeed," added Sally, "but actually they had been around for some time."

"Not like these monsters, though," countered Frances. "These things almost won the war single-handedly for Germany. Why, they were sinking more ships than the allies could replace."

"Actually, it was their unrestricted use of . . . "

"You said a mouthful there, young lady. I was on the *Titanic* when it was torpedoed. Killed nearly 1200 people—civilians—men, women, and children. We sank in just eighteen minutes."

"How did you manage to survive?" asked Sally.

"I was a young man then," answered Frances. "The blast threw me overboard and I clung to debris and paddled my way to shore. Luckily, we had just left New York harbor and were only three or four miles out to sea. I was more fortunate than a lot of folks."

"I must admit," said Micheals, "the sinking of civilian ships did help push us into war with Germany."

"I hope you enjoyed the story, folks, but I see some old friends over in the corner and they're motioning to me to come and eat with them. It's sure been nice talking with you, though."

"He seems like a nice guy," said Sally, "but I hope he doesn't order bologna."

"What do you mean?" asked Micheals.

"Well, it seems to me that he's full enough of that already," she laughed.

What did she mean?

81. Verdun

"You certainly have a beautiful country," said Professor Micheals as he surveyed the scenery from the hillside cafe overlooking the Verdun battlefield. "It's a shame such beauty had to witness such slaughter in World War I."

"Indeed," replied his host, Mr. Jacques Pétain. "It was this battle more than any other that made my grandfather a hero."

"Do you mean that General Henri Pétain was your grandfather?" asked the professor.

"I certainly do," answered Pétain. "The Germans attacked in February, 1916, expecting to crush our forces under the general in a matter of days. Instead, the battle lasted eleven months and ended with the repulse of the enemy."

"Yes, it was a victory for the allies," said Micheals, "but it was at great cost."

"Almost one million were lost here, my friend," said Pétain, the emotion beginning to well in his eyes. "All those men, cut down in the flower of youth. War is a terrible thing, but so is the loss of freedom. So many have died defending it. You Americans know well the sacrifices necessary for being free."

"That we do, Jacques," said Professor Micheals. "We've given much, time after time, to defend our rights."

"And also the rights of others," added Pétain. "We couldn't have won here at Verdun without you. Your General George McClellan was a superb commander who handled his troops well in battle. American men and material might well have been the deciding factor in World War I, and they definitely were in World War II. The world owes you a great debt."

"I deeply appreciate what you've said, Jacques, but I feel that I must correct one little error in our conversation."

———————————————————————

What was it?

82. A Peace Treaty

"We seem to have a difference of opinion here," smiled Professor Micheals as he surveyed his American history class. "Mr. Charlie Jackson thinks that the Treaty of Versailles was a good one, and Ms. Julie Ames feels that it was a terrible treaty. Perhaps we should let the two of you present your own viewpoints."

"That's fine with me," said Julie, "because I know what I'm talking about. The treaty took away all of Germany's colonies and forced her to accept sole war guilt. It further prevented her from being armed while all her enemies had all the munitions they could want. I'd hardly say that a situation like that would help ensure world peace. Germany was stripped of her national pride. No wonder Adolf Hitler had little trouble in rallying the people behind the Nazi party. They were the ones who promised to return Germany to a nation of strength."

"I hear what you're saying, Julie, but you aren't taking a few things into consideration," countered Charlie. "The territory she lost was transferred chiefly on the basis of nationality. That means that the areas she lost were primarily inhabited by people of another nation anyway, and they simply rejoined their country of origin. Her colonies were turned over to the League of Nations, with the goal of their eventually becoming free. Germany was disarmed as a start toward world disarmament—an idea still kicked around today. Furthermore, it created the League of Nations, a forerunner to our United Nations. I think this was a good treaty."

"The main thing it was supposed to do was to keep war from ever happening again," said Julie, "and it certainly failed at that."

"I don't think any treaty, then or now, could guarantee world peace," said Charlie. "The purpose of this treaty was to end World War II, and it did do that rather well."

"Now hold on," interjected the professor. "This thing is getting a little out of hand. Both of you have made some good points, but one has made a mistake."

What is it?

83. Solo Flight

"I enjoy St. Louis very much every time I get to come here," said Sally to the professor as they left their plane. "It's a shame we won't be able to go sightseeing this time."

"I know what you mean," said the professor, "but we've got to be back at Central this evening."

As they were going through the airport lobby, Sally noticed a small airplace hanging from the ceiling near the entrance of a souvenir stand.

"What's that?" she asked. "That model plane looks familiar."

"It sure does," replied the professor. "Let's take a look."

"Isn't this a replica of Charles A. Lindbergh's plane, *Spirit of St. Louis?*" Sally asked the man behind the counter.

"Sure is, lady. It's a model of Lindbergh's famous plane named for this very city. We thought it would be an attention-getter for our shop here."

"It got our attention right enough," said Micheals. "What are you selling?"

"Oh, the usual stuff you'd find in any airport gift shop," said the proprietor. "We've also got loads of "Lucky Lindy" memorabilia. You see, he was a hero of mine. That's why I call my shop the Lone Eagle Gift Shop. I figure it's the least I could do for the first man to make a nonstop solo flight around the world."

"Lindy was quite a guy, all right," said Sally.

"He was my inspiration as a young man," continued the shopkeeper. "Being born and raised here I guess I naturally would look up to a man like that. We've got everything a body could want in terms of stuff about the man and his famous flight. I've got a house full of mementos at home."

"It's nice to have a hero," said Micheals, "and even nicer to be able to make a living from him."

"If I were you, though," said Sally, "I'd be sure to keep my facts straight."

What did she mean?

Name: _____   Date: _____

84. A Man with a Plan

"Trouble in Lebanon, terrorist attacks everywhere, Americans being kidnapped. Why don't we do something about it? You're the history professor, Joe. You tell us why we have to endure all this abuse just because we are Americans."

The gang down at the barber shop had been discussing world affairs and were glad to see Professor Micheals come in. They didn't always agree with him, but they did like to hear his opinions.

"Leadership," shouted Bob. "Pure and simple, it's leadership."

"What you mean is lack of leadership," added Harry. "We've got to show some decisiveness and determination before people are going to give America the respect it used to have."

"Sure isn't like the old days," said Will.

"What do you mean?" asked the professor.

"Well, I remember the Depression days," continued Will. "That was the worst time America has ever gone through."

"That's a fact," said Bob emphatically, "and it was leadership that got us through. The country was falling apart right before our eyes and old

Theodore Roosevelt was the glue that stuck it all together again."

"What was it about Roosevelt that made it possible for him to turn the country around?" asked the professor. "Did he have something that Mr. Hoover lacked?"

"Sure did!" said Harry. "President Roosevelt was a strong leader with new ideas. He saw that old ideas had failed, so he tried new ones."

"That's right," added Will. "Teddy gave his 'New Deal' to the American people and we liked what we saw. He identified the problems and developed ways to correct them. Without his plan of attack we would possibly still be in a depression."

"He was a great man, all right," sighed Bob, deep in a state of reflection. "If we could just have a man like that in control now."

"I agree with you on most points," said the professor, "but I feel that I must set the record straight on one thing . . . "

What?

85. Crash Landing

As Sally Jones waited patiently in line for her turn to vote she became increasingly interested in the conversation of the two men behind her.

"You're crazy to vote Republican, Jake," said one man to his friend. "I was there in '49 when Mr. Hoover caused the bottom to drop out of the market. I said then that I'd never vote for another Republican and I haven't."

"Now, come on, Bob! You can't believe that the Republicans caused the Great Crash all by themselves."

"I sure can believe it," countered Bob. "I tell you I was there. President Hoover was one of the richest men ever to hold the office of president of the United States. He got in there and didn't do one thing to help the little man in our country and, in fact, let the whole economy flop. My folks lost everything they had."

"I still can't believe that one party, not to mention one man, was responsible for the crash," said Jake. "It just isn't possible."

"Like I said, sonny, I was there. I remember the Hoovervilles and the Hooverbuggies just like it was yesterday. When something like that happens it's pretty clear where to place the blame."

"People can be wrong, you know," said Jake. "Often things aren't as simple as they appear."

"Well, it was pretty clear to me. Things were great in this country up to the time that Hoover took over. Everybody had good jobs and everyone had money to spend before he became president. It only took him a little more than a year to wreck it all."

"Excuse me, sir," said Sally, "but you say you remember that time well."

"Yes, ma'am, I do," said Bob emphatically. "I remember it all. I was just telling Jake here that I was there."

"Well, sir, I'm afraid your memory might be slipping a bit."

What did she mean?

86. Big Ike or Big Mac

"What's the problem here?" Professor Micheals asked the two students arguing outside his door.

"Sorry, Professor," said Ralph, "Jan and I were just discussing generals Eisenhower and MacArthur."

"Come into my office and let's settle this," said Micheals.

"Yes, sir," they answered rather sheepishly as they took a seat in front of the professor's desk.

"Now," said Micheals. "Tell me what this is all about."

"Well, sir," said Jan, "it started as a result of your last lecture. We are approaching World War II in our studies, and Ralph and I began talking about various generals involved in the war."

"That's right," added Ralph. "Jan says that Eisenhower was a greater general than MacArthur, and I took exception to that."

"There were many fine commanders in that war, and it's often very hard to place one as being better than another. You must remember that each one was in a unique position."

"We realize that, sir," continued Jan, "but Dwight Eisenhower rose from the rank of colonel to General of the Army by 1944. He was made Supreme Allied Commander and personally led the troops up those German beaches on D-Day."

After the war he commanded all NATO forces in Europe, then was president of the United States for two terms. MacArthur never had a string of accomplishments like that!"

"He was our nineteenth president," said Ralph, "and he was a *real* leader. His father won the Congressional Medal of Honor in the Civil War and Mac won one in 1942. He graduated first in his class from the military academy and became a general in World War I. In 1941 he was commander of all U.S. forces in the Far East and bravely defended the Philippines until he was ordered to Australia. He kept his 'I shall return' promise in 1944 when he liberated the islands. He personally received the Japanese surrender and became her postwar administrator. Much credit belongs to him for Japan's remarkable postwar recovery. In Korea he was U.N. commander and won the war for us. He came home to huge crowds and a hero's welcome."

"Both men were truly great Americans and both had great accomplishments," said Micheals. "Instead of fussing about who was greater, why don't each of you research the other general's career and try to discover the mistake that each of you has made today."

What mistakes did he mean?

87. The Vet

"It was too dark for me to see the man clearly," said Professor Micheals, "but I'm sure it's one of these men. The pickpocket went into the crowd at the veterans' meeting, and of all the people in that room only these three were wearing dark-brown pants, the same as the thief."

"I see," said Inspector Holmes. "You didn't see the man who accosted you, but you did notice his clothing."

"That's right," said the professor. "I felt a tug on my wallet, then it was gone. I turned quickly around and saw the back of a man in brown trousers running away from me into the conference room. There was no one else in the vicinity, so it had to be him."

"And what did you do then?" asked Holmes.

"I had just left the meeting and knew there was no other way out. The doors were already chained in preparation to close the building. I merely summoned a guard and had him detain people fitting the description of the thief as they came out. These are the men."

"We certainly are," said Mr. Wilson, one of the men. "I'm late for an appointment and I must be on my way. I was a marine in World War II. I fought on Iwo Jima and Okinawa and I didn't do all that to be harassed by the police for something I didn't do. You'll be hearing from my lawyer if I'm not out of here soon."

"For goodness sake, Wilson," said Mr. Berry, another of the men. "I was at both those places and at Tarawa, too, with the Marines. Your experiences there should have taught you patience."

"That's right," said Mr. Brooks, the third suspect. "You wouldn't be in such a hurry if it were you who had been robbed. I served on the USS Constitution, and if I learned anything during those voyages during the war, it was patience. Why don't you just sit back and take it easy? Unless, of course, you've got something to hide."

"Are you sure it's one of these men?" asked Holmes.

"More sure now than ever. One of these gentlemen just made a mistake that will cost him quite a bit of time. Now where did you stash my wallet, Mr. _____ ?"

***

Who did it?

88. Patton Pending

"I have always been fascinated by these big machines," commented the professor to his two young nephews as they walked among the lines of tanks at the army museum.

"They sure are big," said Daniel.

"Did you ever drive one?" asked Michael hopefully.

"No," replied the professor, "but I've always wanted to."

"There's no other experience quite like it," said a stranger who was looking at a big M60 battle tank. "My name's Bill Coe, and I couldn't help but overhear the boy's conversation about tanks."

"Do you know a lot about tanks?" asked Michael.

"Well, I know something about them," answered Coe. "I drove one for General George Patton in World War II."

"Boy!" shouted Daniel. "Tell us about it!"

"Well, fellows, tanks were first used by the British against the Germans in the Battle of the Somme in 1916."

"Why are they called tanks?" asked Michael.

"The British called them water tanks while they were being built, in order to conceal their real purpose."

"And the name stuck?" asked Daniel.

"Sure did," smiled Coe, "and Patton knew how to use them."

"He won one of the first U.S. victories of the war at El Guettar in North Africa. Is that where you were with him, Mr. Coe?"

"No, I first met him in England while training for the Battle of Lookout Mountain. Patton's Third Army was my outfit."

"Boy!" sighed Michael and Daniel excitedly.

"Patton was one of our best fighters," added the professor. "Isn't there a special section on him inside the museum, Mr. Coe?"

"Yes, there is," replied Coe. "The curator is a personal friend of mine. If you'd like, I'll go ask him if he could let us have a closer look at the stuff inside than you'd normally get on the tour. Maybe you could even get inside one of these tanks."

"That'd be great!" shouted the boys.

"Boy, did we hit it lucky!" cried Michael.

"I can't wait to get into one of those tanks," yelled Daniel.

"We don't have permission yet," cautioned the professor. "Wishful thinking can sometimes let you down. It usually doesn't do any harm to dream, though. Mr. Coe is a good illustration of that."

What did Professor Micheals mean?

89. Terrible Tarawa

Professor Micheals had just finished delivering his address to the annual meeting of the Veterans of Foreign Wars in Washington, D.C. The meeting was now over and the men were milling about in small groups, renewing old friendships and making conversation. As he was preparing to leave, the professor became interested in a nearby conversation.

"Yeah, you Marines had it tough all right, but not nearly as tough as we had it," said one of the men.

"Is that so?" replied another in the group. "When we hit Tarawa, we had to wade several hundred yards to the beach under heavy fire because you Navy clowns couldn't get us any closer. We lost nearly 1000 men taking that little rock while you boys sat safely aboard your big ol' ships and watched the action."

"It wasn't our fault that you guys had it so tough. We did all we could do. We bombed the place for two months before you guys hit the beach. Then, to top it all off we poured in 15,000 tons of explosives before the first man landed there."

"That may be true," continued the Marine, "but it wasn't enough. The planning for the operation lacked a lot, and we were the ones who had to pay for it."

"We were under fire, too," argued the sailor. "At least you boys had a place to hide on the island. When the German battleship *Bismarck* is firing at you, there's no place for cover. That's what we had to face, so don't give me that stuff about how bad Tarawa was for you poor Marines."

"It's still not the same . . . " The argument continued as the professor headed for his car.

"Did you hear those guys?" asked an old salt as the professor left the building. "I guess it'll never end between the Navy and Marines."

"I guess not," replied Micheals. ' There's no sense making things up, though."

What did he mean?

90. Mr. Truman

"Independence is really a lovely little town," said Sally as she and the professor approached the Truman Library entrance. "I wouldn't mind living here myself."

"I'm sorry, folks, but we don't open until noon," the man at the door was saying. "I'm just here to straighten up the place a bit. Actually, I'm the caretaker. Billows is the name, and I sleep in back. This is my home, you see."

"It must be quite exciting living in a place such as this," said Sally. "I'll bet you know everything about President Truman."

"As a matter of fact, I do fancy myself as somewhat an expert on his life. I've held this job for ten years. President Harry Truman was a truly great man. He had to make several of the toughest decisions in the history of our country."

"That he did," said the professor, glancing casually at the truck parked at the side of the library.

"Like what?" inquired Sally, as Mr. Billows eyed the traffic.

"Well, his toughest was probably whether to drop the atomic bomb on Germany to end World War II. That had to be a terrible weight on his shoulders. The firing of General MacArthur in the Korean War was probably the most controversial decision he made. Many people didn't like that at all."

"I'm sure he had good reason, though," said Sally. "What happened to cause it?"

"I'm sorry," smiled Billows rather nervously, "but I must get on with my work. Why don't you come back at noon, and all your questions will be answered."

"Too bad he couldn't have let us in," said Sally. "He was a very interesting man and seemed quite intelligent."

"I agree totally," said Professor Micheals. "He let us in on one thing, though. He hasn't worked here ten years. He's too intelligent to have made a mistake like that. I think we should call the police."

What did Professor Micheals suspect and why?

         American History Mysteries

91. Kennan's Container

Professor Joe Micheals had been invited to help judge a series of debates on American foreign policy being held at Elkmont High School. The Elkmont team had defended the point that our policy of containment in the Cold War years was a logical reaction to Soviet expansionism. Debate on this particular topic was winding down.

"Elkmont, you may now make your closing statement," said the professor to the team.

"It is our belief that George F. Kennan's containment doctrine was a logical and successful policy utilized to halt the spread of communism in Europe and elsewhere," said the Elkmont captain. "The Soviets were trying to extend their influence by supporting Communist parties in several countries. Our policy of containment saved Greece and Turkey from communist control, just as the Marshall Plan saved war-ravaged Europe. Within a few years after the initiation of the plan, most European countries were exceeding their prewar output, and the communist parties there lost ground steadily. Although the allies were unable to reunite Germany in the postwar period, we were able to keep West Germany and West Berlin free. These are just a few of the successes of our containment policy, but we believe that they adequately demonstrate the policy's worth."

"Grant High School, you have three minutes for your rebuttal."

"It is our contention," stated the Grant captain, "that the U.S. policy of containment was unnecessarily harsh and abrasive to the Soviets. Russia was our enemy during World War II, and the policy so eloquently defended by the Elkmont team did nothing but create more tension between us. As for Germany, we're talking about a country that had started the most devastating war the world had ever known. The Russians had lost 20 million people in that conflict and they had no desire to see the same thing happen again, which was at least feasible if Germany were reunited. The containment policy only caused friction between two great powers that has escalated over the years. The result of containment was reactionary responses on both sides to any trivial occurrence, which only heightened tensions the world over."

As the judges scored the arguments, one observer in the audience whispered to her friend, "I certainly hope the judges caught that mistake."

_____

What mistake?

92. Meeting of the Minds

The flight out of Chicago had been delayed because of fog, so Professor Micheals decided to relax in the lounge. There he spotted an old colleague, Dr. Alice Wong, seated at a table by the door.

"It's good to see you again, Dr. Wong," smiled Micheals as he clasped his friend's hand. "It's been a long time."

"Too long!" replied Dr. Wong. "I suppose you're still in love with American history?"

"Yes, I guess I'll always be," laughed Micheals. "Have you seen the headlines in today's paper about the Kennedy Papers theft?"

"Isn't it terrible," said Wong. "If they aren't found soon I'm afraid they never will be."

"That would be too bad for posterity," said the gentleman at the next table. "I don't mean to interrupt, but I couldn't help overhearing your conversation. My name is Jacobs, Sam Jacobs. We all seem to share two things in common: a fog delay and a love of history. I've been teaching it now for fifteen years."

"It's good to meet you, Mr. Jacobs," said Micheals. "Come join us."

"Those stolen papers are irreplaceable," continued Jacobs as he took a seat. "They had never been made public, you know. If they're lost, the knowledge and insights contained in them are gone too. President Kennedy was certainly a brilliant man."

"It's difficult to image all the contributions he might have made had he lived longer," added Dr. Wong. "We'll never know."

"How true," pondered Micheals.

"His accomplishments were many," said Jacobs. "He was a representative as well as a senator. Before him, there had never been a president who was Jewish. Now all this seems forgotten. It really is a shame. Oh well, things may be looking up. They just announced my flight. I've enjoyed talking with you."

"Seemed like an agreeable man," observed Wong as the man went out the door. "But I wonder what he really does for a living."

How did Dr. Wong know Jacobs wasn't a history teacher?

93. The Lost Cause

"It's truly a shame that so many had to die," said one of the men in the group milling around the Vietnam Veteran's Memorial in Washington, D.C.

Professor Micheals was in the Nation's Capital to visit his friend, Senator Mike Brock.

"It was a tragic war indeed," said the senator. "56,000 dead and over 300,000 wounded."

"And all for nothing," spoke up another visitor to the memorial.

"I would hardly say for nothing," said the professor.

"We learned lessons in that war that should be reminders to us for a long time," added Brock. "The men and women who served in Vietnam were as brave and tireless as any soldiers in any war."

"I guess you're some kind of expert," an elderly bystander sneered sarcastically. "The fact is that we lost. Our country was involved in that conflict from Eisenhower's presidency into Gerald Ford's. We had over half a million men in that little country and dropped hundreds of thousands of tons of explosives on it and we still didn't win. It's as plain as the nose on your face why we failed."

"I'm afraid I'm still in the dark," said Micheals. "Why don't you enlighten me?"

"The truth is that our troops just couldn't match the fighting ability of all those Chinese soldiers that North Vietnam used. It's that simple," said the gentleman matter-of-factly.

"Sometimes, sir, the nose on your face isn't as plain as you might think," said Senator Brock.

What did he mean?

94. A Complex Problem

"Yes, Sally," said Professor Micheals, "this place was the beginning of the end for a president. Once the burglars caught here in the Watergate building were linked to the White House, things began to steadily worsen for him."

"Hello, folks!" called a guard rather cheerily. "Can I help you?"

"We were just looking around," said Sally. "Is that all right?"

"It sure is. I'll bet you folks are interested in the break-in of the Democratic headquarters."

"Why, yes, we are," said the professor. "How did you know?"

"Oh, we get lots of people around here who are interested in that. By the way, my name's Martha Banks."

"I'm Professor Micheals of Central University, and this is my graduate assistant, Sally Jones."

"Nice to meet you," smiled Banks. "I'm about to make my rounds. If you'd like, you can come along with me. I was working here when it all happened so I know all about the break-in."

Ms. Banks gave the professor and Sally a grand tour of the whole complex. She also provided them with firsthand information, detailing every event that had even the slightest connection to the break-in that occurred on June 17, 1972.

"You certainly have amassed a wealth of knowledge on the Watergate burglary, Officer Banks," said the professor.

"Well, it's kind of nice to work in a place that is a part of history. Just think," said Banks, "one simple burglary and the arrest of five men led eventually to the removal and imprisonment of key White House officials such as Attorney General Mitchell, and finally to the resignation of President Ford himself. I feel that I owe it to myself and to visitors here to know as much as possible about an event as important as that."

"That is a very good attitude to have, Officer, but you must take care to present facts only," cautioned Sally. "Otherwise, you may cause people to have an unrealistic view of our nation's history."

_____

What did she mean?

95. What So Proudly We Hailed

" 'The Star-Spangled Banner' gives me a thrill each time I hear it," said Sally Jones, "and your band played it magnificently, Dr. Barton."

"Of course they did, my dear. I trained them well," replied the band director rather pompously. "We always put forth our best effort for the homecoming game. It's quite important to have a good show for our contributing alumni."

"The music is stimulating enough," agreed Professor Micheals, "but when you consider the historical events that resulted in such a song, we can appreciate it even more."

"I quite agree, Professor. That's why I insist on all my band members fully researching every piece of music we play," said Barton. "I feel that if they understand the circumstances of a song's origin, they will get a better feel for that song and will be able to play it better."

"That's an interesting theory, Dr. . . . " started Sally.

"For instance," continued the band director, "by researching this particular song, the band members should have been filled with a feeling of patriotism. I would hope that while playing they would have a mental image of the song's author, Samuel Clemens, as he was being held prisoner aboard the British ship that was bombing Fort McHenry. If they could envision 'the bombs bursting in air' as our brave defenders valiantly held on to the fort under heavy attack, then I believe that the same admiration and pride felt by Mr. Clemens will come bursting forth in the music they play—just as it did in the hearts of the boys defending Baltimore. It was that feeling that helped them hold the fort against heavy odds, and a continuation of that feeling that saw them through to the end of that glorious War of 1812. If my band performs with that kind of intensity and pride, we will always be spectacular."

"As I was saying, sir, that's quite a theory, but . . . "

"I appreciate your thoughts on the topic, young lady, but I must go now to arrange the half-time show. I'll see you both later."

"Well, what do you think about that?" wondered Sally aloud.

"I think he'd better let the band do their own research on the songs," replied Professor Micheals, "or we might have a very confused band."

_____

What did he mean?

96. Presidential Candidate

"How is the campaign going, Senator Wilks?" asked Professor Micheals as he entered the room just before the press conference.

"Quite well, thanks," the senator answered. "The press seems to be treating me fairly in every way. Today is another test, though. Sometimes they can change overnight."

"What will your strategy be today?" inquired the professor.

"Well, I thought I'd give the people just a little of my background to start with, then move right into my political opinions."

"That sounds good to me. People like to know about a politician's life and ideals. If they can relate to you in some way, they'll be more willing to listen to you whether they agree with you or not. By the way, what is your background?"

"There isn't all that much to tell," said the senator. "I was born November 11, 1927, in a small town in Ohio. My parents worked hard and sent me to school where I studied to be a lawyer. After that, I became interested in local and state politics and was elected to office. After eight years in state government, I was elected to two terms in the U.S. House of Representatives, then, finally, to twelve terms in the Senate. That's pretty much my story up to now."

"I think it says a lot for you to have achieved so much on your own. So many politicians get into office because of their wealth or the wealth of their family, but you seem to have done it on your own."

"My family has always been behind me. They would have done more, but they aren't rich."

"This all sounds nice, but I wouldn't tell my story in just that way if I were you."

What is the professor talking about?

         American History Mysteries

97. A Friendly Little Campaign

As Professor Micheals and his friends sat in the restaurant waiting for their food to arrive, the conversation turned to politics.

"I just can't believe how ugly our politics has gotten in the recent past," said Dr. Joann Goss.

"Whatever do you mean?" asked Dr. Garry Scroggins.

"I mean these political campaigns," continued Dr. Goss. "It seems that politicians hardly ever focus on the issues anymore."

"That's right," added Micheals, "and I feel it's a shame. It seems to me that there are plenty of issues worthy of debate, but all we seem to get are personal attacks on the candidates."

"Exactly," continued Dr. Goss. "That's what I'm talking about. It's a shame we can't go back to the good old days when politicians were honorable enough to debate issues, and not stoop to spreading rumors and gossip about one another."

"Just how far back would we have to go, Dr. Goss, to reach these good old days?" asked the professor.

"Probably quite a ways," answered Goss. "I'm a medical doctor and you two are historians, so I know you are much better informed than I am in these matters, because you've studied them in detail. I would imagine, though, that in the days of men like George Washington, political parties ran clean campaigns. I'll bet that politics was on too high a level for any type of smear tactics to be used."

"You could safely bet that Washington wouldn't go for anything like that," smiled Scroggins, "but we'll never know what his party would have done."

What did he mean?

 American History Mysteries

98. Family Ties

"Nepotism! There is no denying it this time!" cried Dr. John Morris. "The only reason you are making Davis the head of the American history department is because he is your nephew."

Professor Micheals was horror-struck. He had stopped in at Grumley College to visit Sam Leighton, an old friend and now president of the college. He had never expected to see a scene such as this taking place in Leighton's office.

"What's bothering you, Morris, is that I know just as much about history as you," said Davis smugly. "I haven't taught history in a few years, but it's like riding a bike—once you have it you always have it."

"That's not true and you know it," shouted Morris. "It is a prime example of your faulty reasoning, though."

"Gentlemen! Gentlemen!" shouted Sam Leighton. "This is all getting out of hand. Let's be civilized about this."

"All I want," said Dr. Morris, "is for the best person to head the department. Nothing less will do."

"That is very understandable," said Leighton, "but what makes you so sure my nephew couldn't handle the job? He's had the best education money could buy."

"That's right," chimed in the would-be department head. "There is nothing wrong with following in my relatives' footsteps. Even presidents have done that. John Quincy Adams was the son of John Adams. Benjamin Harrison's father was a congressman, his grandfather a president, and his great-grandfather a signer of the Declaration of Independence. Franklin Roosevelt was Teddy Roosevelt's father, and Franklin, by the way, has been found to be related to eleven presidents by blood or marriage. I just want to continue my family tradition."

"Just a min . . . " started Morris, but he was interrupted by Sam Leighton.

"My dear friend, Professor Micheals, you have heard all of this. Can you help me decide? I'm a physicist, not a historian, and I need the best man for the job."

"If that's true then you can't appoint your nephew," said the professor, "judging from what he just said . . . "

What did he mean?

       American History Mysteries

99. Presidential Term Paper

Professor Micheals sat at the rear of his classroom, listening intently as Sara Allen presented her term paper to the class.

" . . . It is therefore my considered opinion that the founding fathers never intended the vice president to become president in the event of a vacancy in that office. The original Constitution declared that the powers and duties of the office were to pass to the vice president, but no mention was made of the office being transferred. John Tyler, in 1841, set the precedent of the office itself devolving to the vice president. This practice has been followed ever since. In 1967, the Thirty-fifth Amendment officially made this informal amendment a part of the written document."

"Is the vice presidency then vacant, Sara?" asked a student.

"The amendment says, 'Upon a vacancy of the vice presidency, the president will nominate a candidate who will take office upon confirmation by a majority of both houses of Congress."

"What if both the presidency and vice presidency are vacant?"

"In a case whereby both the president and vice president have left their offices vacant, the Presidential Succession Act of 1947 would go into effect. The speaker of the House would be first in line to succeed to the presidency, then the president *pro tem* of the Senate. The secretary of state and the other heads of the Cabinet departments come next, in the order in which they were created."

"Then, Sara, it appears that we could possibly have a president who was not elected to any public office," commented a classmate. "I mean, the Cabinet members are appointed by the president and are not elected by the people, yet they are in line for the presidency."

"That is correct," replied Sara. "I really don't feel that there is any need for alarm, though. We've lasted over 200 years and have made it just fine. Besides, if we ever got that far down the line of presidential succession, we would undoubtedly be in serious trouble, and other controls of governmental powers would probably be making major decisions."

"Any other questions?" asked the professor. "Then let me say, Sara, that you did an excellent job with your paper. You were obviously well prepared and are quite knowledgeable on the subject. You did make one little mistake, though . . . "

What?

100. A Better Letter

Answering letters from people interested in various aspects of history is one of Professor Micheal's favorite pastimes. His staff handles much of the work load because the professor is so busy with other activities. Today, though, he has time to drop in and see if any really interesting requests have come his way.

"How does the mail look today?" he asks as he enters the workroom.

"Oh, it's mostly the usual," answers Jack Webb, the professor's office manager. "I do have a few that you might be interested in."

"Okay, let's have them," says the professor as he sits down at his desk.

"Here's one from a student in middle school. He's writing a book about the presidents of the United States. He says he has gathered much information, but would like to know who were our tallest, shortest, and heaviest presidents. Also, were any children ever born in the White House?"

"Another is from a young lady who wants your help in securing the war record of her grandfather. It seems that he was in the battles for Guadalcanal and Iwo Jima. She would also like the names of the men who raised the flag on Mt. Suribachi. She thinks he was one of those men, but doesn't know for sure."

"Another writer," continues Jack, "requests information on the Korean War. It seems that his father was a member of General Patton's tank command in that war. He wants a copy of the war records so he can prove the fact to his friends."

"Two of these letters can be handled rather easily through various research methods," says Professor Micheals. "I can send a reply to the other one right now. That writer either had poor history teachers or slept through class too often."

Which request was that?

100A. Who Is Responsible?

"Another American hostage taken in Lebanon. When is all this going to end?" commented Sally as she and several friends sat by the pool.

"I think it's a sad commentary on the state of America's image abroad," added Grady Snyder. "Things like this didn't happen to Americans until lately. Our determination to stand up for ourselves has dwindled to nothing during the Reagan years."

"And what's that supposed to mean?" asked Dan Green, the famous Wall Street broker. "Are you saying we've suddenly gone down the tubes as a world power?"

"What I'm saying is we used to react to such confrontations with a little backbone. We never let anyone push us around," continued Snyder.

"Now wait a minute," said Sally. "We've tried to get our allies involved and to seek diplomatic solutions to all these problems, yet . . . "

"Yet, it isn't working," interrupted Grady. "These Third World countries think we're only a paper tiger, and they're laughing in our face. We haven't made one single attempt to use our vast military powers to try to resolve any of these issues. In my opinion, we're just plain scared."

"You don't know what you're talking about, Grady," said Dan, "and I can prove it."

———————————————————————

What did he mean?

100B. The Party

Professor Micheals found himself in the middle of a very interesting discussion. Governor Mary Ellen Morris and Mr. David R. Brown, the Democratic party national chairman, seemed to be at odds over the governor's support of the Republican candidate for president.

"I simply feel, Governor Morris, that the Democratic candidate deserves your support in this crucial contest," said Mr. Brown.

"And I feel differently," answered Governor Morris.

"But the Democratic party has for years been the liberal party. We're the party that tried to change the status quo and get women into more responsible government positions. Now, just when we need your help most, you turn your back on us. That isn't fair."

"I'm not turning my back on the Democratic party, Mr. Brown," replied Governor Morris. "I am simply following my conviction that the better candidate for president of the United States is the Republican candidate."

"But you've heard all the criticism of the Republicans' record on the issues of women's rights under the Reagan presidency, and you're telling me that you will support a man who is dedicated to continuing those policies for the next four years. I just can't believe it," said Brown.

"Sometimes criticism isn't completely justified, Mr. Brown," continued the governor.

"It is justified this time, Governor Morris, and you know it," answered Brown rather excitedly. "It was the Democrats who ran a woman as its vice-presidential candidate against Ronald Reagan and the Republicans in 1976, and it will be the Democrats who'll finally achieve equality for women in this country. You, of all people, should understand how difficult a job that is. That's why I thought we would be able to count on your help. The Republicans haven't made one attempt to achieve sexual equality, yet they get your support. I find that quite ironic."

"Your argument might be more persuasive if you stated the facts correctly, Mr. Brown," answered the governor, "and I resent your misrepresentation of President Reagan's efforts on women's rights."

_____

What does she mean?